Mud Season

Center Point
Large Print

**This Large Print Book carries the
Seal of Approval of N.A.V.H.**

Mud Season

Ellen
Stimson

CENTER POINT LARGE PRINT
THORNDIKE, MAINE

This Center Point Large Print edition is published
in the year 2014 by arrangement with
W. W. Norton & Co., Inc.

The text of this Large Print edition is unabridged.
In other aspects, this book may vary
from the original edition.
Printed in the United States of America
on permanent paper.
Set in 16-point Times New Roman type.

ISBN: 978-1-62899-022-5

Library of Congress Cataloging-in-Publication Data

Stimson, Ellen, 1962–
Mud season : how one woman's dream of moving to Vermont,
    raising children, chickens and sheep & running the old country store
    pretty much led to one calamity after another / Ellen Stimson. —
    Large print edition.
pages cm
Originally published: Woodstock, Vermont :
    The Countryman Press, 2013.
ISBN 978-1-62899-022-5 (library binding : alk. paper)
1. Stimson, Ellen, 1962– —Family. 2. Vermont—Biography.
    3. Vermont—Social life and customs—21st century—Anecdotes.
    4. Vermont—Social life and customs—21st century—Humor.
    I. Title.
CT275.S755A3 2014
974.3´044092 D—dc23

                                                    2013038388

Mud season is a period in late winter and early spring when dirt paths such as roads and hiking trails become muddy from melting snow and rain. When the muddy paths and roads are traveled over by wheels, they develop ruts. It is regarded in some northeastern states within the United States, like much of New England, as both a curse and a blessing, because, although it is generally a messy time of year, it is an interlude between the standard tourist seasons of summer (hiking), fall (leaf peeping), and winter (skiing).

Mud season occurs only in places where the ground freezes deeply in winter, is covered by snow, and thaws in spring. Dirt roads and paths become muddy because the deeply frozen ground thaws from the surface down as the air temperature warms above freezing. The snow melts, but the frozen lower layers of ground prevent water from percolating into the soil, so the surface layers of soil become saturated with water and turn to mud.

It is also characterized by giant puddles on the side of paved roads, from large piles of snow melting with no place to drain off to. Sidewalks, parking lots, driveways, and all other surfaces become a muddy mess. Clothing is etched with drops of muddy spray, boots are covered in a layer of mud . . . and the backs of pantlegs display a telltale spray pattern. The mud droplets are stubborn and cannot be removed with normal laundering techniques.[1]

1. Wikipedia contributors, "Mud season," *Wikipedia, The Free Encyclopedia*,

http://en.wikipedia.org/w/index.php?title=Mud_season&ol did=554334106 (accessed June 20, 2013).

This is the mostly true account of a few seasons of our quirky Vermont life. But memory is a curious combination of events, feelings, and wishes. I figure my recollection is about 83 percent true. Maybe 78 percent in a couple of places.

My Uncle Winston always said that we should never let the truth get in the way of a good story. I took that advice to heart. My kids have always made it a habit of correcting little details in my storytelling . . . tiny things, it has always seemed like. Well, this time they can't. I've already said that it was only mostly true.

So there.

—ELLEN STIMSON
Dorset, Vermont

⇒⇒ Contents ⇐⇐

☞ Prologue ☜

You don't know me, so here's a few things you'll probably need to know. I'm a midwestern girl who has always been pretty lucky—successful too. I don't say that as any sort of brag . . . it's context. The events of this book take place during the early days of my life in Vermont. As a good disclaimer might state, past performance does not predict future results.

If you've ever taken a kid to the beach . . . or Disney World . . . and had to explain, at the end of a long, happy, sunny day, that we can't always be on vacation, then you are one step ahead of me. My family and I thought it might be fun to make that actually happen . . . living in one of those beautiful places where we vacationed and maybe making a living there, too.

We were half-right. Well, mostly half.

I love Vermont, and in some ways the more-worrying of our early days here made it all the clearer that there was no place quite like it. There is no more naturally beautiful place I have ever been, and I have been to a bunch of them. We never left. We still love it. But if you find yourself planning to move here, I maybe could offer you a couple of tips.

≫ Chapter One ≪

Vermont

Falling in love makes you do strange things. Maybe you only order a salad at dinner rather than the lobster drenched in butter that you actually wanted, or you start reading that pretentious novel you've owned for years but never thought anyone ever actually finished, after the love interest mentions that he really enjoyed it. There are cravings, too.[1] I once drove to a grocery store in my bathrobe at 4:00 a.m. to get some purple candles for a breakfast date. Candles that I am pretty sure I forgot to light, and that I am completely certain the man on the other side of the table never noticed. And when you fall in love with a place . . . Well, when that happens, you may do strange things on a slightly grander scale. Or anyway, that's how I apparently do it.

It all started as a simple, great date. I had been married to John for a while, and we had two little kids. One was so wild, he might as well have been raised by actual wolves. The other one woke up mid-conversation every morning. She would open her eyes and say, "And then," beginning anew

---

1. Mostly lipstick and shoes, in my experience.

every day. Benjamin and Hannah would grow up to be caring, successful adults. At least, that was the plan. At the time, they were what you hear people euphemistically refer to as . . . a handful. There was a lot of sleep deprivation back then, so great dates were few and far between. We were young, and broke a lot of the time. When we had the money and time, we also had kids who needed a fun diversion more than we did. Mostly we rummaged through purses and pockets to come up with enough change for dollar night at the movies. Sometimes we had cheeseburgers and chocolate malts on our front porch. There were plenty of carnival rides, homemade popsicles, and tent houses in the living room. We had a really terrific treehouse out back, and come summer we made ice cream by the barrelful. Kid-centered activities we had in abundance. Plenty of those. But, quiet candlelit dinners . . . meandering adult conversation? Not so much.

Those were the sweet, if always a little tired, years. But in 1994, John and I finally went off on a long New England weekend by ourselves. It was the first time we'd ever traveled without the kids. We were thrilled at the idea of sleeping late, not having to apologize for the inevitable messes our kids made in restaurants, and maybe even showering together. We were so excited that we held hands in the hot, dirty airport parking lot and felt that it was somehow romantic.

We flew out late on a Friday and landed in Burlington, Vermont. It was early October, and I was yearning for my first peek at the famous autumn foliage, being something of an autumn kind of girl. The first flash of color, followed by a sad, windblown ending, always appealed to my need for drama. I loved the sexy, bawdy nature of fall. Even our little midwestern parks were transformed by the riot of color. For one or two brief weeks, the humidity faded and was replaced by temperatures that favored cozy sweaters, just before the first freeze. St. Louis is supposedly a town with seasons. In fact there are two—summer and winter. Summer lasts from April until October, winter, from November through March. Spring comes for a day or two, followed by the summer humidity. But still, there was always that brief weekend interlude called fall when all was right with the world.

For a fall fan, Vermont has real appeal. It practically invented the whole autumn vibe on the tourism calendar—sweet rolling mountains, sugar maples blazing with red, yellow, orange, and even purple. There are always boutique farmers at roadside stands selling cheese, bread, bunches of beets, and hot apple cider; wildflowers displayed in old jelly jars; countless fairs exhibiting everything from antiques to merino sheep. If you love fall, Vermont is for you.

I was a little nervous and wanted everything to

be perfect on this, our first trip away alone together. I am kind of excitable during the best of times, and this trip was carrying a big load of expectations, so I may have been even more keyed up than usual. During the flight, I must have said to John dozens of times, "I sure hope it's still light when we get there. Do you think it will still be light when we get there?"

It wasn't.

We drove the two hours to Killington in the dark. I began to panic.

"I don't think the leaves have turned yet. Oh no! We're too early. Find a radio station with the foliage report, will you? They must have stations that will tell us where the color is. I think the mountains look green. Do these damn mountains look green to you?"

"They look black," he deadpanned. "It's nine o'clock."

John is . . . calm. Someone around this family has to be. Personally, I come from a long line of overreactors. Luckily, as Steve Martin once famously said, it seems to be diminishing with each successive generation. There is even some faint chance that my someday-grandchildren might actually be normal. If they are, it will be because of John Rushing altering the gene pool. He makes me laugh and he remains calm. It's a good combination.

After checking into our inn, late and tired, I

fell asleep disappointed. John woke me in the morning, calling from the balcony. He seemed to be using exclamation points. He hardly ever uses exclamation points. I immediately wondered if he'd seen a bear. There are bears up here.

"You'll need your cape, it's cold."

So . . . probably not a bear.

My wool cape wrapped around my nightgown, I walked out into the spectacular splendor that is a Vermont autumn. The mountains around us blazed every shade of orange you can imagine. Who knew there were so many different oranges? There were big bright reds, too. Lots of yellows. Purples. And the light. Oh, the Vermont autumn light.

To say that the light is golden doesn't begin to cover it. It is really more of a soft orangey color. Is it the reflection of the sun on all those leaves? I still don't know, but I do know that the light dripping over everything cast a glow that made everything prettier. It felt like a blessing. I think maybe the word "sublime" was invented just for that light. I'd never seen so much autumn in my life. It was everywhere. Now I knew what all the fuss had always been about.

It even smelled different here. There was a heady cold snap in the air and the scent of pine was everywhere. I was giddy. It was love at first sight—I felt dizzy. I had the sense of the world shifting—the same feeling I'd had after giving birth to my children. I have always thought that one of the great reasons to be alive is that you never know what's coming around the next corner, what grand passions are going to change everything. From that moment I, at least subconsciously, knew that I had to live in this place, which, for a few weeks each year, is the most beautiful spot on earth. The rest of the year it is merely *one* of the most beautiful spots on earth.

I'd read *Heidi* as a little girl, and I longed for fresh goat's milk in the morning with hunks of cheese and bread, and a life just like the storybook. These Green Mountains were smaller and rounder than Heidi's Swiss Alps, but somehow they were more comforting—more nurturing. I felt like I'd come home.

The idea of folks "falling in love all over again" may seem silly. But sitting on the hood of our rental car at a roadside farmstand in the cold sunshine, feeding each other maple pickles with Vermont cheddar, and sourdough bread, and sipping apple cider, necking and giggling like teenagers, John and I fell in love all over again with each other, and for the first time with this place.

It took nine more years and another baby before our move became reality, but in retrospect, that was really the moment when we decided to live in Vermont. There on the hood of a car, eating, kissing, and adoring that beautiful fall day.

● ● ●

Our family had spent our whole lives in the Midwest. And they were good lives, too. Our days were full; and if the joy often came in the repetition—kids' games, familiar restaurants, a favorite theater—at least it still came. But we longed to live in a beautiful place.

Now, growing up in the Midwest with my family, I had certainly learned the value of good work. Sometimes the work was hard, sometimes it was smart, and sometimes it was just lucky. I've always been able to see a way to build businesses. At first those were other people's businesses, and eventually they were my own. Hard work, luck, and a handy knack improved our economics. And with that improvement we began to travel. We would plan out the trips as a family project, and put aside cash throughout the year. The planning was a big part of our lives. The travel was joyful. San Francisco, Italy, Chicago, Florida, New England. But when we returned home, one of us would inevitably feel let down; so we'd immediately begin planning the next destination.

Wherever we visited, we played the "What if we lived here?" game. It was on one of those trips (an unforgettable time with all five of us in Tuscany)[2] when we thought about what it would be like to

---

2. So, really, I can blame all of this on *Under the Tuscan Sun.* Well, okay, maybe 78 percent of it.

live in those old hills. We imagined grocery shopping at the open markets and traipsing across the countryside with grapes and tomatoes and farm-fresh cheeses.

Our daughter Hannah, then about twelve, wondered out loud, "Okay, but we always play this game. Can we *actually* live wherever we want?" Hannah likes things organized. She brings order out of chaos wherever she goes. Our family gives her plenty to work with. Like most of her rational questions, this was a good one.

Benjamin, our eldest, chimed in, "Mom, you fly everywhere for work anyway, and Dad hates St. Louis summers . . ." Benjamin loves a good adventure. So this seemed like a fine idea to him. Benjamin has never walked quietly, when shouting, spinning, jumping, and climbing were options. As a teen, this was sort of endearing. At nine months, when he climbed on top of the refrigerator to see what was there, it was terrifying.

John asked, "Wouldn't you guys miss your schools?"

Turns out that, sure they would, but it might be worth it to live somewhere "really good," whatever that was. So with a bit more discussion, we decided that the answer to "Can we live wherever we want?" was, in fact, "Yes."

We'd lived in and around St. Louis our whole lives. So we asked the question. "Would we choose to live in the Midwest 'with intention,' or were we just living there 'by habit'?" It was nice, rambling, vacation conversation. Only then the answer came really quickly, too.

Eli hopped in with "No way! I want to live in Florida by Typhoon Lagoon." He was nearly six. And a theme park would, obviously, add to his overall life satisfaction. Or maybe an ocean. Eli loves the beach. Every time we would visit a beach, Eli would, of course, do all the splashing, swimming, sand-castling stuff, but he would inevitably end up staring, for what must have been hours, into the waves where they met the sand. Hours. So, living close to an ocean . . . or possibly a theme park with a nearly-ocean in it . . . might be best.

I thought I should probably have a say in this. I am one of the adults, after all. So I contributed that, "I have always wanted to live somewhere that is, by any objective standard, beautiful. I like St. Louis, sure. I like the food and our schools, our friends, our house . . . but I would sure like to be able to see the mountains when I drove home, rather than another Meineke muffler shop. It would be fun to walk on a beach on any given Tuesday . . .

"But what about Grandma?" I added in what I thought was a responsible afterthought. My mom still lived in St. Louis, and she was nearly eighty.

Hannah chipped in, "Um, do we even like Grandma?" Oh boy. This might not be such good vacation talk after all. And then John sweetly added, "When we were dating we always wanted to live in Elsah or someplace like it. Remember?"

That I did remember.

Elsah is a little turn-of-the-century village in Illinois that sits atop the bluffs over the confluence of the Missouri and Illinois Rivers. With about fifty or so full-time residents and one sweet little café, it was as close to New England as you could get in the Midwest. And we loved New England.

Autumns are pretty in the Midwest. There are gobs of maple and oak, and those Elsah bluffs were a long, uninterrupted line of blazing color in October. St. Louisans "go to Elsah and see the leaves." John and I had spent one fall and winter falling in love in one of its inns.

So, some of us would choose mountains. Some would choose the beach. We loved big, gorgeous cities like San Francisco and New York, too. Benjamin thought, at the time, that being in a city was what he needed. He craved coffee shops and record stores. But he was also open to adventure. We loved Cape Cod, where we had spent so many happy July days, but one place that consistently came up was Vermont. John and I had told the kids all about it years earlier. And we had been back many times since as a family. We'd climbed Mount Tom, been to the dog trials at the Annual Sheep Festival, wandered through countless fairs, and followed dozens of rivers. Each of us had our own warm vacationy feelings about it. We imagined we could have our rural mountain idyll and still be a morning's drive from both the sea and New York City.

"Well, if we could live anywhere, why don't we?" said Hannah. She's the thinker and planner. She couldn't figure why we weren't already living in Vermont if we all wanted it. It was a fair point. Why, indeed?

What, after all, did we value? Was living surrounded by natural beauty really and truly vital to us? If it was, why did we continue to live in a place that we traveled away from every time we had the time and money? However, once we got home to St. Louis, the questions began really revealing themselves to us. Did we mean it? Were we serious? Where would we live in Vermont? How would we make a living? What about schools?

We quickly answered yes to the important questions. We meant it. We were, apparently, serious. The rest of the questions we answered one by one, as only city people can—romanticizing the experience from a thousand miles away.

We had gone shopping at the Life Store in a big way. People who know me might tell you that I have a bit of a short attention span. That's probably only if they are being exceptionally kind. In a job interview, I could describe myself as someone who likes new challenges. But, really, the attention span is why I have bought and sold, or started, so many new businesses. I actually can't hold a job like normal people do. I, um . . . I get a little bit bored. My less kind teachers called it "flighty" when my papers wandered and meandered far afield of the given assignment. My mother had said, about five hundred times, "Oh, Ellen. Not again. Well, I suppose when you get older maybe you will finally know your own mind, and then you will settle down."

She was still saying it.

So the Life Store became my happy euphemism for the time to do something fresh, punch up the tempo, change things up, and pick something—anything—new. Things not working out in your current life? Go to the Life Store and pick out a new one. A life that fit you better. Maybe one in a nice bright color. Possibly Vermont Fall Orange?

This time, of course, we were all in it together. This was the Life Store for real . . . and for five. So we picked a new life. We picked rolling mountains, roadside streams, and wooded knolls. We wanted to gaze at the sky and the stars this time around. We had our fill of really good (and surprisingly cheap) Thai food in our old neighborhood. We aimed, instead, for supper beside a stream and our morning coffee in the woods, and to get the kids out of the shopping malls. Benjamin was thinking adventure. Eli planned to live outside all year round. Hannah longed to ride bikes wherever she wanted and not have to worry about her purse or "those weird guys in the park." John decided that instead of becoming winded from jogging beside bus fumes, it would be nice to be exhausted from uphill climbs through ever-greens. We wanted bonfires in the backyard every night. We wanted to wake to birdsong rather than the rattle of garbage trucks. So we chose Vermont.

Vermont—a little blue state known for its hippie ice cream, beautiful views, and liberal politics. A rural state, Vermont "boasts" only three malls— mostly in Burlington. They were the last state to allow a Walmart to open. Big-box stores are rebuffed in favor of little village country stores, where you can still get everything from a light socket to bird food to local cheese, while you find out the baseball scores and argue local politics. There are no roadside billboards in Vermont. And it's a state with way more cows than people.

Deciding to move north was surprisingly easy. Obviously, we had already made that decision years ago. It was just a matter of recognizing it. But that left finding a place to make these new lives.

Our realtor, Willie Hersom, drove us through a surprising amount of Vermont while we looked for that place. We must have seen thirty-seven houses over the course of several trips (thirty-seven? Yes, just the thirty-seven) with Willie and his black Lab. They were a sweet pair. Willie's dad had owned the real estate office until his recent death. Willie was likely taking on way more at his age than either he or his parents had planned. Of course, taking over a business at a young age is a bit overwhelming on its own. Willie might not have anticipated quite what I would be like as a client. I had . . . ideas. But Willie had decided that he could possibly sell us a house. The Lab didn't venture an opinion.

We were leaving a big old Victorian in the Midwest with gorgeous walnut and oak woodwork in every room. I had told Will that we wanted woodwork. This led to his showing us some odd modern houses with unfinished beams, which wasn't what I had in mind at all, so I sent emails with longer and longer explanations. Woodwork, yes, but woodwork with character. Something old . . . distinctive. I might have used the word "glorious." We were looking for an old house in the woods, or possibly the village, with views of the mountains, four or five bedrooms, a big gourmet kitchen, and lots of porches—cheap. How hard could it be?

Will was a patient and fun companion. It seemed that he and the dog were glad to be out of the office. And as any good Vermonter would, he was making sure we were the right sort. The actual sale was his second priority.

"Smell that? Manure. They just fertilized the fields. I think it smells good. Bothers some people. You guys care?" We assured him that this was exactly what a morning should smell like.

He passed along stories of a family who had recently moved there and was now writing letters to the local paper asking the town to consider streetlights. "We have stars. We don't need street-lights. Some people move here and then want to change everything. Now, why do you guys think you want to live here, again?"

Stars and manure, Willie. Stars and manure.

He seemed to think we would be passable Vermonters, and perhaps, just possibly, he could sell us a house. Finally, on one of our trips, his mother suggested that we look at a couple of places in Dorset. Presumably, thirty-eight was the charm.

We pulled into the village to look at a house next door to a country store. The house had been temporarily converted into an art gallery, but it was tough to imagine living so close to a place with gas pumps and busy local commerce. So we skipped that one. We liked the look of the town, though. Quintessential New England. The next house was his mom's suggestion. It was just around the corner and up a little hill. But since we were already in the village, we thought a little explora-tion wouldn't hurt. Willie came along, pointing out and explaining the sites along the way.

We were on Church Street—the main street . . . okay, the only street . . . in the bustling downtown that is Dorset. Church Street's historic district featured a beautiful old inn, aptly called the Dorset Inn, at one end and an old Gothic church about four stories high at the other. There was a grassy, flower-planted area with park benches, and there were old Colonial houses with dark-green shutters throughout. The houses sat back from the street and were obviously well tended and much loved over the last two hundred years.

Across from the inn was the other significant anchor for the street—really for the whole town—Peltier's. Peltier's was a country store that looked like it might just have been a Hollywood stage set. The sign hung from an old wrought iron hook—ESTABLISHED 1817. It was said to be the oldest continuously operating country store in America. It was three stories high with a steeply old-fashioned pitched roof. It had a wide front porch and flower boxes blooming under all the windows. It was utterly charming.

There was a bell above the door, and big fat jars of licorice and penny candy lining a row of shelves. There was an ancient brass scale that told your weight and horoscope for a penny. There were pictures going back to the nineteenth century hanging next to shelves stuffed with toys, homemade bread, and groceries. The floors were old oak, waxed to a high sheen, with square nails securing them. There was a wine room, coffee bar, truffle oils, and shelves of good-looking pasta. And cheese. Lots and lots of wonderful local cheese from the goats and cows just up the road.

"Mom, I'm starving." Hannah had joined me for this trip and was making a good point. It had already been a big day, and . . . well . . . there was all this food.

"Let's get a hunk of this good cheese, honey, and how about a baguette. And then we can nibble in the car. Willie still has a few more houses for us to see." These trips had been packed with school visits and house hunting, so there wasn't a lot of time for restaurant dining.

But choosing the cheese . . . that was a puzzle. I am something of an avowed bibliophile and a devoted foodie (with the backside to prove it). I sometimes play a little game when I am drifting off to sleep. If I were stranded on a desert island, with only one book and one food—what would I bring? Books are complicated. Food, a bit less so. Cheese and chocolate usually vie for the position. I can amuse myself for a long time imagining just which cheese might make the cut.

Now here in this country store was a whole case filled with local cheeses, some wrapped only in brown paper with a handwritten note:

MAGGIE'S CHEESE

Maggie is a 4-year-old Toggenburg and her milk has a high butterfat content. Her cheese is always sweet and this little crumbly goat cheddar has been aged for three years. Maggie's cheese is a lovely sort of yellow and extra creamy. $7.00

Okay, Maggie's went into the bag. And this:

EQUINOX

Made from our free-range organic goat herd in Pawlet, Vermont. Just like its mountain name-sake, the Equinox is an aged strong cheddar. Real cheese lovers will come back again and again for the satisfying tang of the Equinox. $8.95

Hell, I could spend a hundred dollars on just cheese.

In the end, we settled on three cheeses, and grabbed a baguette and some chocolate soda pop before heading to the register. I kept thinking, "Here . . . We could live here!" in breathy, happy thought bubbles. I could easily imagine walking to the store to choose our supper. It seemed a very European lifestyle. Pick good, fresh, local food and carry it home for the evening meal. My romantic fantasies were piling up fast. These people knew how to live.

There was a smiling man in the back who chatted us up. I wondered if he and his wife owned the store. I could imagine them up early, making the coffee and sitting out on the porch before the customers came. What sweet lives they must have.

So we sat on one of those park benches on the green—they called it a green. Oh my. And we ate our cheeses. This was quite a village. After lunching and romanticizing, Hannah and I set out with Willie and his lovable Lab for the next house.

The house sat on four acres. It was just up the hill from Peltier's, but far enough away to feel separate from the village. There was a wooded knoll with a wonderful winding trail that led to an old stone tower built for the Astor children in another century. There were four porches wrapping the house. Itself. The front porch had lovely views of Spruce Peak, a little point along the Taconic Ridge. The steps were crooked little ruins, but they could easily be rebuilt. That gracious porch was topped by a balcony, where Hannah and I imagined a slew of languid sunbathing afternoons drinking lemonade while reading trashy magazines. There was a side porch, on what had originally been the front of the house, and a screened porch on the woodsy side, which might, with a wall full of windows and a little heat, become my favorite napping spot. John and I hoped to take most of a year off to settle into these new lives. Our fantasies were rich with possibility. This place even had a name. Manorside. It seemed perfect.

Once Willie brought us inside, we did see a few challenges. The kitchen had dark, dirty beams that looked like rotting railroad ties. But surely those could be boxed in oak or walnut. A little effort and they could be restored to an old glory. The kitchen space was a little smaller than we'd hoped, but a good carpenter could bump out the wall, add a mudroom for all the ski parapher- nalia we envisioned acquiring . . . maybe even a banquette, lending the place an old French farmhouse kind of appeal, to go along with its wonderful window. Both sides of the window swung out, and I could imagine calling the children in to supper.

And there was a library. Okay, so it didn't have bookshelves yet, but it was in all ways perfect for some. It was a gracious, twenty-four-by-twenty-four-foot space, with a fourteen-foot-high copper tin ceiling up above. This had some poorly done repairs that, in the fullness of time, would turn out to be a thrifty papier-mâché made from leaves, old newspapers, and glue, which was painted to match the original tiles. But surely we could find some antique replacement tiles and easily restore the ceiling as well. Upstairs there

31

were five bedrooms, in addition to the little guest nook behind the library, for a total of six. The master matched the proportions of the library, and I pictured myself learning to weave on the big old loom I'd just found on eBay. The house, with a few minor repairs, was grand. And of course we'd add the accoutrements for a gourmet kitchen, but that would involve little more than switching out the stove and the fridge and maybe adding some local slate countertops.

This place was perfect. Perhaps, with our being under the effects of all that beauty, and possibly all that cheese, Willie had sold us the house his mom had recommended. With just a few renovations, this house—this village—would be a start to our new, magnificent Vermont lives.

Plus there had been that whole little armed robbery thingy, which kind of sealed the deal.

≫ Chapter Two ≪

The Armed Robbery

We told all our friends that we were moving to the mountains of Vermont for the natural beauty. And it was true. But of course there was also that little armed robbery thing. I say thing . . . really it was more an armed robbery misunderstanding.

I generally did the weekly grocery shopping on Friday evenings when we lived in St. Louis. On the night in question (the procedurals always say "night in question," right?), I had a full cart, and was waiting my turn to check out. I was behind a man buying a couple of those giant-sized cheap beers and some cigarettes. He was looking a little unkempt and very worn out.

The cashier rang up his items, and he handed over his debit card. This was back before the days of swiping our own cards, so in addition to the purchase he asked for cash back. The checker ran his card, and got that wrinkled-brow look of checkers everywhere who recognize that this transaction isn't going to go well. She turned to the worn-out customer and explained that his card wasn't working.

I took an unnecessarily intense interest in the

magazine rack. I mean, if I was looking at a magazine I couldn't possibly be overhearing the argument that was developing. I kept busily looking at the magazines as his voice got even louder and demanded that she try the card again. The cashier called her manager—an altogether helpful sort—who swiped the card, handed it back, and said, "No, sorry, it's been declined" as he walked immediately away, leaving the cashier and the guy both looking pretty dejected.

"Look, why don't you try the ATM? It's right there," the cashier suggested, wanting to settle this as soon as possible.

I offered that, "Hey, I'm in no hurry. I'll just wait."

The customer stepped over to the ATM (back then there were no keypads in the actual checkout lanes), punched a few numbers, and had no better luck there. He came back to the checkout line muttering about "those stupid machines," before doing a rather unexpected thing. He pulled out a gun and said he needed twenty dollars.

Now, I don't know about you, but I believed him. I was no longer looking at the magazines. My brain registered two basic principles: Gun = bad. Running away = good. So, like any right-thinking person in the grocery store on a Friday night with a cart full of groceries facing an angry gunman, I immediately turned and ran out of the checkout line. This whole thing had gotten out of hand and I was not interested in being there if it got any worse.

Now, I say I ran away. Mostly I *attempted* to run away. You see, I had a little problem. There was a tiny Vietnamese woman behind me in line and she was pushing a huge cart full of groceries that was blocking my way. I turned sideways and tried to scoot by her, but as it turns out she wasn't paying attention to what was going on and had, apparently, *actually* gotten engrossed in the magazines. And I have . . . I might have mentioned that I have, er . . . um . . . well, a rather ample backside. So, what happened was that it . . . that is, my derriere . . . got . . . um . . . stuck . . . yes, okay, so . . . stuck, between her cart—Did she really need all that stuff anyway? I mean, she was tiny. Who was going to eat all that?—between her cart, as I was saying, and the gum. Sort of wedged, actually. Cart—ample backside—Juicy Fruit. This was not my best night.

I have to admit, and I'm not proud of this, that I forgot about the gun for a moment and found myself trying to wriggle around so that nobody would see that I was stuck. There was a guy with a gun three feet away, and I was embarrassed about my butt. I cursed (rather dramatically) and imagined getting shot because of my big butt. There would be headlines in the *Post-Dispatch*. Local TV news coverage. My mother's church group weighing in, as it were, on how none of this would have happened if I'd just said no to that second helping of cheesecake.

Meanwhile, back in the non-butt-related drama, the cashier had frozen. Nobody else in the store seemed to notice what was happening. How do you not notice armed robbery, I wondered? But the guy with the gun was just standing there, bouncing nervously from foot to foot, and the cashier was panicked—frozen. And then I saw it.

I was facing the back of the cashier in the next line over, trying to unstick my behind. That cashier, blissfully unaware of the robbery or my . . . derriere difficulty . . . opened her drawer to give change to the person in her line. So there I was, staring at a pile of cash, stuck between gun and gum. The choice seemed pretty simple. I reached out, grabbed a handful of twenties, turned back toward my line, and handed the wad of cash to the hapless robber while . . . right, well, I might have been screaming, "HERE! TAKE IT! RUN!!!"

Which he did.

Promptly.

So my cashier started to cry. The other cashier started screaming that she was being robbed—I guess it's easy to be vocal about these things when the guy with the gun has already left. And pretty soon our buddy the manager came back. The police were called, and the story tumbled out.

"Well, yes, of course I handed him the money. He had a gun . . . and I couldn't . . . well, not exactly . . . couldn't entirely escape . . . So, you know, it seemed like the only thing to do."

They invited me to the manager's office. They may have used the word "accomplice" a time or two. Or three. Oh for goodness' sakes. I mean. Accomplice? Really?

I called John, who was (alarmingly, I thought) not as surprised as you might want your husband to be when he finds out that you are being accused of armed robbery. In his defense, he explained that he'd been married to me a long time by then. I'm not sure how to feel about that.

John headed to the store after calling a lawyer to meet us there.

Eventually, after more retellings of the butt-cart incident than I was entirely happy about, one of the older policemen realized that I, obviously, had nothing to do with the armed robbery of two forty-ounce malt liquors, a pack of cigarettes, and a handful of twenties. Besides, the guy had swiped the card several times while he was in the store. If it wasn't stolen, then they had his name. If it was stolen, then they had him on store video at the very least.

I was released, and found—to my horror, if we're being honest—that the staff had taken my cart for abandoned and restocked all of my groceries while I was chatting with Kojak about the size of my ass. I had to do the whole grocery list over again.

We went out for dinner that night.

I skipped dessert.

But let me just say that not every goddamned amply proportioned shopper is an accomplice to armed robbery. Some of us are just thinking quickly in a stressful situation. Still, my family took great joy in pointing out over dinner that now we *had* to move to Vermont. Clearly, I was wanted by the authorities . . . or had fallen in with a bad crowd . . . or didn't need to clean my plate after all. Comedians, the lot of them. Next time, I'm just getting dogs. With dogs, at least you know what you are getting.

So first I sold my business.

I didn't start out planning to sell it, actually. I'd invested a lot of myself into making this thing work. So the plan had been to move to Vermont and run my end from there. Only, my business partner and I, wildly different personalities, struggled to find gentle common ground. We always had. We could look at the exact same problem with the exact same set of facts and think up wildly different solutions Every. Single. Time.

She was a good person. I was a good person. We just naturally disagreed. The notion of moving to Vermont and leaving that ever-present conflict behind quietly began to take hold.

One day I was talking to our realtor, Willie, on the phone and he mentioned that his mom was holding an estate sale in what would soon be our new house. He was suggesting that I might want to let her know if I wanted any of the furniture that was still in the house.

At least, I think that was what he was suggesting. What I was hearing was "estate sale."

I loved antique furniture almost as much as I loved books and the book business I would soon be leaving. Estate sale.

I could practically smell the furniture wax. Maybe this could be my new business? Sure. Why not? Maybe I could start flying to Paris and buying up a shipping container's worth of stuff. I could mingle it with local New England treasures and create some kind of blended estate-sale business.

What a lovely Vermonty life that would be.

Or maybe I could buy a truck and travel around to auctions and estate sales all over New England. And then I'd partner with a Vermont realtor to stage the furniture inside old houses that were for sale . . . maybe host national estate sales aimed at tourists. Hey, maybe I could also partner with a local inn to set up weekend antiquing junkets for vacationing shoppers from New York City and Connecticut, bringing them in for my monthly estate sales.

The dreams began to accumulate.

One day I mentioned to John over coffee that perhaps I should offer to sell my partner my half of the business and do something new when we got to Vermont. Mr. Steady Calm Rational Man suggested, "Why don't you think about it for a while, Ellen. See what bubbles up."

Fine.

Probably good advice. So I took it.

That was at about eight o'clock in the morning. At ten, I offered her my half. By noon, I had hired a lawyer to begin the negotiations.

John wasn't as surprised as you might imagine.

Things began to fall into place fairly quickly then. Christmas was coming up, and if I was going to sell my part of the business anyway, I really didn't want to be stuck in that office all of December, when I could be planning my house rehab and wrapping presents. So I quit going into the office while we negotiated, and spent my afternoons at design showrooms with books of fabric and color swatches instead.

We all agreed that this was the best use of my time.

At least, I'm sure we would have agreed, if it had come up.

It's true that I might have been taking just a tiny little risk here. I mean, yeah, I was fantasizing pretty wildly about what my Vermont Life would be like. But the truth is that I'd always been lucky with these sorts of decisions. I'm an intuitive person. I can size up a business situation pretty well, and this seemed to make sense to me. We'd already put the business on good footing. My partner could handle things from here forward. Possibly better than she could with me involved. She knew what she was doing. Sure, this was a quick decision, but all my best decisions were. Selling the business would give me a solid start on a future in New England. We could take the money from the sale and pour it into the house, and possibly get a head start on new businesses.

John and I had career-swapped early in our marriage. When the kids were little, he held down a variety of PR writing jobs and I stayed home. I nursed each baby until they were about two, and then we would switch roles. John would stay home doing freelance PR while taking care of the kids. It was a good arrangement, and in this way we raised our children together. I had a knack for sales, and along the way I had the good fortune to work for one of the nation's premier book wholesalers, the Booksource, in St. Louis. After graduating from that entrepreneurial environment, I bought my first business, Unique Books.

In a now-repeated family story, I came home one day and said to John, "I think we need to own our own business, honey, and I found a library wholesaler that I think would be just about perfect. What do you think?"

You know, in the way you might mention that the tires on the car were showing a little wear. Or that it might be nice to buy a new rug for the living room.

"Wow," he responded. Probably reasonably. "Where is it? How much will it cost? Will you move it to St. Louis?"

He asked smart, responsible questions, while I wrote business plans and ran cost projections. I began making sales calls on local banks to persuade them to lend us the money. The numbers were so big and our bank account was so little that it all seemed more like Monopoly money than anything real. Still, apparently this was how it was done. You convinced the Banker that financing your purchase of the B&O Railroad was really an investment in his future. It's not like you're picking up that overpriced Boardwalk or anything. This was an important part of the infrastructure. Railroads were a great investment.

Well, that, or you convince the bankers around town that you are pretty good at selling books and that it wouldn't be totally insane to loan you just enough to buy a distributor and relocate it across the country. It might have been easier to sell him on a railroad, but with a Chance card and a lucky dice roll I won them over.

John's last very reasonable question on the day we closed on those loans was, "You don't think we'll wind up living in a truck stop, do you?"

I kissed him. He kissed me back, and we signed on the dotted lines.

Besides, truck stops aren't so bad, really. They have showers and all the beef jerky you could possibly eat. But, honestly, I never imagine anything going wrong. It's just not how I tend to see the world. If the chances are pretty decent that things will work out, then imagining bad things happening doesn't make any sense. This particular character trait is not always a good thing, but that time it turned out to be right, and now here we were five years later selling Unique Books, which by almost happy accident meant we could finance this new visit to the Life Store.

Now, I had started to imagine my sweet new life in Vermont. I imagined big swaths of time without that pesky job. And I had another idea. I could take up weaving. It was going to be cold in Vermont and I imagined needing piles of capes and big cozy blankets woven with yarn I would buy from local sheepherders. Without the tedium of an "actual" job, I spent hours online reading about looms and yarn. I wondered if that cute little country store in the Dorset village sold local yarn. On eBay there was a turn-of-the-last-century loom that had been made in Vermont: it was, obviously, destiny.

I signed up for classes starting in January.

And so our house rehab began in earnest. The months passed in a happy blur.

One of the ironies of being me is that I crave change but I'm not good at transitions.

John and I had only moved three times since we had been together. There was the first time, when we moved in together. That one almost didn't count, right? We were too young to know anything about anything. And we had way less stuff back then.

Way. Less.

When you are in your twenties you can pack the night before and move house the next day using high-octane coffee on exactly no sleep. Still, I was not very good at it even then, truth be told.

I pulled that all-nighter thing during that first move, and paintings were stuffed in the backseat of my car without wrapping or packing in bubble wrap. Bubble wrap . . . it seemed like too much, really. Also, I didn't exactly have any at the time. Lamps teetered on my front seat, and every necklace I owned hung precariously (and noisily) from the rearview mirror. A bunch of our friends had helped us load everything else into a rented truck, and we repaid them with A&W burgers, fries, and root beer. There may have been some other kind of beer by the end of the night.

We caravanned the truck to our new home and started marching boxes inside. My friend Lauren helped me unpack the kitchen. Can I admit something now, some twenty-five years hence?

Oh what the hell, it was twenty-five years ago. So, at one point Lauren opened a box and found the dirty dishes that I had taken out of the dishwasher as we were packing. Well, it was an all-nighter. We were tired. Lots of coffee. You get the idea. My mother would have died.

Anyway, we looked at the box, laughed a bit, and then . . . okay, so yes . . . my mother was there that day so we did the only reasonable thing. We hid the box until she left. Then, like mature adults, we put them right into the new dishwasher. Well, of course we did.

Move Number Two took us to a sweet little house in Edwardsville, across the river from St. Louis. Our kids would spend their early years in a giant sandbox we built out back, underneath a treehouse that was bigger than our bedroom. We spent ten years in that house, having suppers out on a wide front porch with a bright red swing. I gave birth to both Hannah and Eli during our time in that little house. It was a good house.

John and I had been raising Benjamin in our Park Avenue apartment in the heart of the urban renewal that was happening in St. Louis. It was a hip neighborhood, but I was carrying Hannah, our second child, and was suddenly feeling decidedly less hip. We were craving the coziness of Edwardsville, with its town band concerts and its pond in the middle of the city park. And it would be the first home of our own.

There was already more "stuff," though.

The books alone took dozens of boxes. We're readers, and books . . . well, they just sort of seem to accumulate, right? Then there was all the kid stuff that we had somehow gathered for Benjamin. And the baby stuff left from Benjamin or picked up in anticipation of Hannah. Oh, and our music. So many albums left over from young adulthood that just couldn't be parted with. And the burgeoning collection of foodie accoutrements. The potato ricer was important. It was. Also, it needed to be packed . . . unpacked . . . but probably not washed immediately.[1] So there was a lot more stuff to move, which made this transition a bit more complicated. Well, that and the whole subletting thing.

You see, we had to move two whole weeks before we could close on our new house. The folks we were buying from weren't ready to move yet. They needed two weeks. We couldn't afford the rent on our apartment and the mortgage at the same time. The people we were buying from were not ready to move. We had a two-week gap. So we packed everything,[2] and moved it into my mother's house, which just happened, at that moment, to be for sale and so it was empty.

1.We were learning to cook for real at this point, so accessories were important. And on this move there would be no dirty dishes in a box. Really. Promise.

2. Okay, John did.

There we stored our accumulated lives, while we stayed with her in her new little two-bedroom apartment. For two weeks.

Two weeks in a two-bedroom apartment. My mother, who would never move boxes of dirty dishes, John, Me, Benjamin, and our cats and dogs.

Two cats.

Two dogs.

On the second day I had to go on a business trip. At least there would be one less person in the house. That night, I called to tell Benjamin goodnight. John coughed and cleared his throat a lot. He said that he had something he needed to tell me.

"Are you sick? You sound sick." All that coughing. Must be from the move.

"No, I'm fine," he assured me. "Everything's fine. Well, mostly fine. Except . . . um, your mom left."

"Left?" I didn't quite get it. Left? Like, the country? Whatthe?

"Well," he continued, "she said I should take the cats to her old house. You know how they were racing around last night? Apparently they kept her awake. She decided that they should stay at her old house with the furniture. She thought I should just go over and feed them but leave them there."

"Our cats? Alone in that empty house?! Is she

out of her mind?" My mother and I have a complicated relationship. And these were tight quarters, but c'mon. She knew about the cats when we decided to do this. And on top of that, it had only been one night. I mean, really. One night for the cats to get used to a new apartment, and she was already evicting them? Would she send her grandson packing tomorrow for playing too loudly in the morning? I mean, the nerve.

"Where is she? Just lemme talk to her!" I might have raised my voice just a bit.

"Don't worry," John soothed. "I told you, she's gone. I explained to her that I wanted us all to talk about some . . . possible alternatives. I said you'd be calling in a bit, and why didn't we all talk about it then. I thought we could problem-solve it together."

"Yeah, so then what?"

"And then she sort of . . . well, she set her mouth, packed a bag, and said she was moving out."

I come from a long line of overreactors.

"I'm sorry, honey." John had probably realized at this point that he would often find himself in these situations, but I felt like I should apologize anyway.

"Look, I am not as crazy as she is. Our baby might even be normal." It seemed like something he should know.

"Don't worry. Benjamin and I just made a bunch

of popcorn and we're going to watch a movie. It's actually nice here. And the cats seem much calmer now, too."

So Move Number Two was sort of god-awful in its own unique way. As a pregnant mom-to-be I was useless in the toting and packing. Okay, as it turns out, being pregnant had nothing to do with my being useless at moving. But that was what we told ourselves at the time.

Ten years later, for Move Number Three, there were fifty boxes of books, and I started crying when the first roll of packing tape came into the house. We began to face the truth. I was not a good mover. I hate transitions. I am not a naturally organized person, and I was neither brave nor cheerful.

After a decade in Edwardsville, we'd decided to move our family of five back across the river to St. Louis. We were headed to a beautifully restored Victorian on a wide tree-lined boulevard. My job during Move Number Three was to stay out of the way. It seemed the best choice.

And now here we were, barely five years later, doing it again. Sure, this time we were moving to Vermont, a long-cherished dream, so it was different. We were thrilled to be able to make it happen. We were going to New England. We would be shopping in country stores and having our morning coffee beside rivers. The dreams had been piling up for a while. But then we had to call the movers. The day they came to inventory the house, which included books (158 boxes), art (seventeen paintings that needed to be individually wrapped, packed, and shipped . . . with bubble wrap this time rather than in the backseat of an overcrowded car), the bursting kitchen with its food processor, juicer, fryer, beloved KitchenAid stand mixer, John's precious espresso machine, and dozens of gadgets we played with every day, the collection of auction-house antiques and flea market chic that made up our country style, alongside the upholstered furniture, the beds, the kids' stuff, and . . . well . . . just all the junk of five lives . . . okay, I started to cry. That is, apparently, my job when we move. About two weeks before the big day, I start crying, and I barely stop till we get to the new place.

The nonstop crying only starts at the two-week mark. But for a month before the move I warm up with intermittent crying. Like vocal exercises . . . or stretching. The day the movers came, I was in charge of negotiating the price. As I've said, I've got a good head for business, and I figured this was a sale like any other. So I was walking around the house with the estimator, trying to get the best deal. One minute I was hard-negotiating pricing and getting bids. The next I was running my hand over the mantel and remembering our first Christmas in the house . . . sobbing.

"Ma'am?" the very disconcerted mover asked.

"Ma'am, are you all right? I know it's expensive. But maybe we can get you a discount. Ma'am?"

John overheard us, and gestured to the poor, befuddled man to accompany him into the dining room.

"She's okay," he told him. "Let's go into the other room and look at the rest of the bid. She'll be back with us in a few minutes. She . . . uh . . . she doesn't move well."

"Oh God. I am so sorry." The mover blanched. "I must have bumped into her when we were counting those shelves. Does she have MS? I've got a cousin with MS. It can be very painful." To his credit, the estimator was horrified that he had injured me.

"MS?" It took John a second. And then another moment to figure out how to answer that.

Oh.

"Um, no," he answered. "Not exactly." Though, to be fair, he may have wondered if there was a diagnosable condition amongst the bawling. "Let's just take another look at this bid."

Meanwhile, I was wailing away in the living room.

This didn't happen every day.

At least, not at first. It was really very intermittent. I was still relatively sane most days.

Until about that two-week mark. Then it was pretty well constant. I walked around in my old ratty robe with Kleenex coming out of every pocket. My eyes were watery and my face was blotchy. Meanwhile, John . . . well, John moved us.

He ordered boxes. He bought tape dispensers. There were giant rolls of bubble wrap in every room. He had a staging area in the library, and the dining room table was covered with labels and schematics for the new house. Every kid's room had an allotment of labeled boxes and trash bags. Some were filled with old, torn, and broken things headed for the dump. Others were labeled "Goodwill." Some of the boxes of books were labeled "Donation Books" and would be dropped at the library as once a week he culled and weeded our collection. There were boxes of old toys that were taken down to the Salvation Army headquarters. Old dishes and furniture were headed there, too. Things were labeled and stacked neatly in the vestibule. And in the library, the fiction collection was boxed alphabetically and the nonfiction was packaged by section. There was food lit, travel lit, regular travel, biography, memoir, politics, feminist thought (from my relevant days), John's enormous history section,[3] and a collection of kids' books that could have been the opening-day stock in a nice kids' store. He was a master. And as I wandered from room to room watching as he packed up our old life and planned for the next one, I behaved like a regular mental patient.

---

3. I married an intellectual.

John was unfailingly kind and calm.

"Hey, El . . . ?" He always started with a gentle question, as he took my emotional temperature.

"Hon, do you want to take these old Nancy Drew books to Vermont?" This seemed like a completely reasonable question. Little did he know.

"Nancy Drew?! Nancy Drew was my very favorite and closest childhood literary friend. Hannah and I have loved reading those. Nancy Drew? Are you kidding me?!" My voice was hitting an uncomfortable range . . . for all of us, probably.

"I know," he would add, "but this set is pretty shabby. I just wanted to make sure."

Okay, to be fair, they *were* shabby. The covers were old and torn. The pages were foxed and the spines were cracked.

And I wanted them. I wanted all of them. In fact, I had just that moment decided that I was going to take a book-restoration class because I. *Loved.* Those. Books. And I intended to take them with me to my grave.

I may have explained this in something other than my inside voice.

"Okay, sweetie. Just checking."

Into a box they would go.

His equitable nature and calm presence were really pissing me off. How dare he be so sane, when my whole life was in a box? We were leaving all of our friends and family and everything we had ever known! We didn't even have jobs or any idea about what we were going to do in Vermont. What exactly was wrong with him, anyway? In fact, come to think of it I was sure we were all making a horrible mistake.

Then I remembered that they didn't have streetlights in Vermont. I had never been a great night driver.

"John, ohmygod! John, look, I think we have made a terrible mistake. I think we may just have to face it and walk it all back.

"John?! John?? We cannot move. We cannot!

"I am afraid of the dark!

"John?!!"

My voice may have gone up just a little tiny bit at that point. "Shriek" would have been too strong a word. It wasn't really a shriek. Well, hardly a shriek.

John's method was to keep the patient as comfortable as possible and hope for the best.

"Okay, hon. Here's a cup of hot chocolate." At this stage he hardly registered surprise at the . . . emotional . . . tone of my conversation. "Now, could you possibly reach over and hand me that tape roll?"

I'm not good with transitions.

On Moving Day Number Four, the three-story garrison brick house in St. Louis looked pretty forlorn, with bare windows and stacks of boxes, as everyone worked to load up the truck. John, Benjamin, and Eloise, our Bernese Mountain Dog, would be making the journey by car. Eloise was too big to fly, but just right for the backseat. So father and son (and dog) would drive across the country, leaving one life and beginning another the old-fashioned way. They would cross the states seeing and feeling the distance we were putting between our old and new lives.

Hannah, Eli, and I were flying with our daughter's best pal, Elle—who planned to help Hannah unpack—with Sophie, our decidedly unamused fifteen-year-old cat,[4] and our Cairn Terrier, Stuart, who was small enough to carry on. Actually, at a stout twenty-two pounds, Stuart barely missed the twenty-pound cutoff, or maybe not so barely, actually, but we stuffed him into a small-sized pet carrier (he was, I guess, more of a medium, but a gentleman terrier doesn't make an issue of such things) and let him poke his head out every time the flight crew and grumpy-looking passengers turned their heads to glare away in disapproval.

---

4. The scene at airport security when TSA told me that I had to take Sophie out of her carrier and walk her through the screening, which included her (just to be clear) screeching and clawing the whole way, had made me just a teensy little bit upset. Covered with hair (cat and human) in a wild blur of sweaty curls, we proceeded with this whole "destiny" journey thing. Next time I'm driving . . . with the dog.

We landed in Albany and drove to Vermont from there. The plan was to stay at a B&B for a day or two while the renovators put the finishing touches on our 1830s farmhouse.

Actually, the real plan had been to meet the movers and start unpacking. Unfortunately, my contractor let me know a couple of days earlier that there was a teensy little, hardly worth mentioning, really, bit more work to be done. And so the local inn had taken our reservation instead. We would fill three rooms. Fortunately, they were all near the back entrance. We had hidden Stuart and Sophie during check-in, and had plied them with bones and tuna, respectively, to gain what we prayed would be their quiet complicity.

On the day we drove to the new house, it was a breezy seventy-something degrees in Vermont. The whole village smelled loamy and fresh. The sun was shining, and we were all excited. We'd heard the town church bells ringing old hymns at noon, as we'd carried our suitcases into the inn. The bells rang every day at noon and five. How simple and sweet, I thought, to live your life to the rhythms of those bells. I imagined gathering provisions at that cute little country store, cooking supper, and stepping outside to stand beside the rosebushes I'd plant next to our new picket fence, perhaps holding a cup of tea as I listened and reveled in our new life here in this gentle old place. It was pretty good as fantasies go.

Then we drove up the lane.

There were thirteen men, with hammers and cigarettes, leaning out of every window. Rather, they leaned out of big gaping holes where the windows were supposed to be. The windows, as it turns out, had just been delivered, and blue tarps fluttered in the wind. Hmmm.

We'd hired a cleaning crew who were supposed to have the place shiny and sparkling when we arrived. It seemed that they had swept a few piles of sawdust, but had given up in the face of new messes being made faster than they could clean up the old ones. So it wasn't exactly sparkling.

There was our Viking cooker, the one I had been dreaming about for months (eight burners and a convection oven) gleaming in the fading Vermont sunlight in the middle of the meadow. I had imagined bonfires in that meadow, but not really my shiny new cooker. It had been delivered on time, but the electricity and gas weren't ready yet. Somehow it had been shuttled to the meadow.

Of course, the grass in the meadow and everywhere else too was about four feet high. While we were still in St. Louis, we'd hired a grass cutter to take care of this, but we later discovered that he'd apparently had an issue with the new picket fence and had stopped coming . . . weeks before. At least the grass hid all the cigarette butts.

We jumped out of the car and I began gushing about the woods, sending the kids on a scavenger hunt to hide my distress. Sometimes a fig leaf is enough. The late-afternoon light was fading and bats were circling our heads. I'd never seen a bat up close before.

My contractor, Kevin, stepped out of the house and welcomed me, handing me a stack of invoices and saying they were running a little over and could he please have another ridiculous sum of money in the morning. One of the guys saw me looking at the bats and said, "Wait till you see the coyotes." I thought about how I'd just sent the kids into the woods. Looking through the invoices, I remembered the insane figure we'd already paid. At least it came with bats and coyotes included. And possibly mountain lions. We had mountains, right? Did we have the lions that came with them?

Then, as you might guess, or maybe not, actually, the police cruiser drove up. I mean, yes, I had sort of been involved in a minor bit of armed robbery, but that really hadn't been my fault. I was not normally the kind of person who attracted police attention. I wasn't.

The officer got out and sauntered my way, asking if I "was the lady who hired these fellas." Stuart was barking, all these "fellas I hired" with their hammers and their cigarettes had disappeared, the kids were wandering around the darkening, coyote-infested, mountain-lion-probable mountain, and I began to wonder, not for the first time in my life, just exactly what had I been thinking?

Back when we had started this process, I had been caught up in that detailed fantasy that featured months of choosing wallpaper and paint, and fun goodbye parties with all of our friends. I had started calling Vermont contractors, explaining how we needed some bookshelves in our new house and a little help with the kitchen and a few other repairs. Several came by for a look. They began sending me bids. Well, I say bids. They were like no other bids I had ever seen before. These were bids of breathtaking proportion. They would bankrupt us.

Clearly, we would need to make some adjustments. And we did. Or I did. I swear I did. In the end, the rotten porch steps stayed, along with the dicky electricity and the bathrooms that left your knees touching the wall at strategic moments, and the ceiling (no one really ever looks up much anyway), and the screened porch had had screens for a hundred years that worked perfectly fine, thank you very much. We were left with a putting-a-kid-through-college bid that covered book-shelves and plugging in the stove. Worst of all, the timeframe for completion was eighteen months. We were moving in a little under eight. Two of us have asthma, so living in a construction site could literally be life-threatening. We were in trouble. But then I remembered Kevin.

Kevin was the funny St. Louis contractor with a cell phone in each hand, a big cigar, and an even bigger truck. His dog's ashes rode in a little vessel on his dashboard. Kevin was a sweet guy with a big crew that he flew down to Alabama every year to work on his rental properties. Kevin had done beautiful renovations on our St. Louis house—the one with windows . . . and a kitchen . . . and no coyotes. I wondered if he could be tempted to bring his guys to Vermont? Maybe so.

I called him. We flew him to Vermont and wooed him with dinners by the fire and long wandering drives around the countryside. We casually took him to the house on the second day. It seemed wrong to mention windows, walls, and beams on the first day. But on the second day, a casual mention seemed reasonable. I talked about the bookshelves. I chatted about the kitchen. We had wine on the balcony. Lots of wine. Eventually we made our way through the dining room, past the rotten steps, through the family room with its bowed walls and wavy floor. I had a punch list that I revealed slowly through the week. You can't just drop a list like this on an unsuspecting contractor. They have delicate sensibilities.

Eventually, we found a house to rent for his crew and started planning the work shifts. Eight would sleep while eight worked. Everybody would get an eight-hour break, except for the ones who wanted overtime. He could knock it all out in six weeks, starting the April before our move, working round the clock, six days a week. Kevin knew that some of his crew were tired of traveling, but he thought he knew where he could hire on some extra folks. The price tag he suggested was only unthinkable, but as the three of us sat on a quilt where the terrace would one day be, we figured, what the heck, we would only do this once. It would be worth it. In retrospect, the notion of bringing an entire construction crew to Vermont and housing them for weeks seems a little extreme. It was certainly expensive, but I can tell you that the bids from local contractors took years off my life. Those were numbers that you hear about on *Marketplace*. In reference to the national debt. Plus, hiring locals would just take far too long. Besides, what were nest eggs for, anyway?

Now, eight months later, there was a state trooper in my yard suggesting that one of these charming nicotine clouds had driven off without paying for his gas at the local country store—the charming country store with the chatty couple behind the counter, and the cheese. Oh dear. Also, the driver was alleged to have been weaving. Had my loom arrived already? So the store owner had reckoned the driver'd had a few beers. I remembered that Kev was a recovering alcoholic, who often hired guys just out of the program that had saved him. I suddenly knew where he'd found the extra guys.

The trooper asked me if I knew who had been driving the truck he described. Kev ran over and apologized. He offered to run right down to the store and pay for the gas. Before the trooper left, he was smoking one of Kevin's cigars and seemingly accepted that the fellow had just "forgotten" to pay. In this teeny little village, with only a few hundred year-round residents, this was big news. I heard it myself the next morning at the coffee counter in the quaint little village store. A very nice bearded fellow with a giant cup of coffee told me all about the new people who had hired those yahoos who had stolen some gas. If his cup size was any indication, then he intended to stay a while and tell the charming anecdote a few more times.

That day at lunch, I heard more about these ridiculous new people. Apparently, I was being taken for a tourist who could appreciate the humor. It seems these new people had hired a bunch of foreigners to remodel their house, thinking themselves too good for the local guys, who surely could have used the business. These foreign guys bought up all the beer in the store and one of 'em had met a pretty local girl and come in looking for "rubbers."

The guy behind the counter reported to a room full of people, "I told him we didn't have any but

I could order him some . . . be here by Wednesday if he could wait. But I figured if he was asking then he would be needin' 'em 'fore that, so I also told him where there was a drug store that carried 'em. Then I called up that girl's brother and told him to keep an eye out. Don't know if he ever needed 'em after that."

I felt a little bit queasy.

That night, back at the inn, John and Benjamin showed up with our dog, Eloise. Eloise was a Berner, and, given the lack of windows at the house, she had to sneak into the inn with Sophie and Stuart. Luckily she was like Nana in *Peter Pan* and would reliably and quietly look after all of us. Stuart was a little less reliable in the quiet department, but surely, I figured, Eloise would keep him under control. I could depend on our faithful Eloise more than just about any humans I knew. Furthermore, I now knew that I couldn't possibly trust my dogs around this work crew. Or mountain lions. The reunited family had dinner at the inn and planned our explorations for the next day. Later that night, I whispered to John a few of my concerns: cost overruns, delays, troubles with the law. He reminded me, in the way that he does, that we'd expected some of this. He stroked my hair and said surprises went with the territory amid all this change. I went to sleep happy, if maybe still just a little bit nervous.

Little did I know.

• • •

Since Eloise was one of my best friends (dog or human), it never occurred to me that I was doing anything much wrong by sneaking her into the inn. Stuart, our probably-medium-sized Cairn, I worried about. Stu didn't like change, and in tense times his terrier side asserted itself. But Eloise? Of course not.

The kindly innkeepers had given us permission to bring Sophie inside. Sophie had been described to them as "an elegant, aging cat." She was all of that, sure. But "elegant" was also just about right for Eloise as well. Yes, she weighed 110 pounds. She had a boxy Berner build. It's true she also loved cheese rinds, which every farmer's market cheesemaker seemed to offer her. So perhaps there were seven . . . maybe eight . . . extra pounds that weren't, strictly speaking, a result of the Berner build. But Eloise walked gracefully through the world. She seldom barked unless she had something really important to say. She was certainly a more refined guest than any of the rest of us. And all this sneaking around we were going to have to do—taking her out the back door, tiptoeing down the hall, looking around the corner—felt a little unseemly. I may have resented it. On her behalf, of course.

Eloise was an early riser. In the morning, I checked out the hallways and took her out as Stuart and the rest of the family slept on. John had gotten in late after the cross-country drive and needed a little more sleep. Of course, I wanted more, too, but he had just driven a thousand miles, so he won the toss. Eloise greeted the day with good cheer. I tended to get cheerier after coffee.

So I was barely bumping along that morning when we got back to the inn after Eloise had sniffed every flower and been admired by all the early-morning walkers in Dorset.

We eased in through the back door, and I peered down the hallway before proceeding to our room. Now, it should be noted that in that hallway at 6:00 a.m. all the rooms looked exactly alike. Sure, the doors had numbers on them, but they were little. And they were in a fancy script. So it was hard to tell what they actually said in the muted hallway light. Still, even without coffee, I knew that my room was at the end of the row.

Rooms in this inn didn't have coffeepots. Coffee was served down in the public rooms. I could have tromped down to the public rooms in my sweats, but I thought a nice quick shower would be just the thing. Then I would be refreshed before heading out for coffee.

Eloise and I quietly walked into the room, where John was still sleeping; I could see his form under the covers. And so I tippy-toed over to the bathroom hallway, stealthily undressing in the dark. I figured I'd turn on the bathroom light when I got in there.

Now, the bathroom door was closed, which I might have thought odd. Only, I didn't. No coffee yet. No shower yet. Not exactly at my sharpest. I opened the door just as the lady inside was emerging.

She screamed. Really loudly, as I remember it.

I screamed.

Eloise barked.

And the man in the bed sat up and said, "Whaaa?"

Two of us were certainly naked. One of us was under covers, so his state couldn't be determined. I said something brilliant then. Probably, "OHMYGOD OHMYGOD," as the woman, panting now, wrapped a towel around her middle.

I grabbed for my clothes. The man scrambled for his glasses, but dropped them on the floor. I bent to give them to him and then thought better of it. Adrenaline is apparently almost as good as coffee in the morning.

"Holy hell, I think I have the wrong room," I helpfully said. No kidding, El, I thought. Really? Congratulations on that quick thinking.

"OHMYGOD, I am *so* sorry," I blurted as I tried to put my bra on—backwards. I gave up on the bra and just pulled on the sweatshirt. "OHMYGOD . . ."

Eloise had stopped barking and was patiently waiting by the door.

The man, having found his glasses, sat up in

the bed with the covers pulled around him, calmly taking in the scene. He finally spoke.

"Huh. Do they allow dogs here? Linda, maybe we should have brought Ralph."

I went back to my room. We could go out for coffee. After I showered. In my room.

Willie called. Remember Willie? Nice kid. Has a black Lab. Sold us this lovely house that was going to bankrupt us? Willie thought we'd want to know that the landlords for the workers' rental place had stopped in, and they were a little bit upset. The landlord's wife, a woman of delicate sensibilities and keen eyesight, had seen some . . . er . . . things poking out from under the couch . . . and underneath one of the beds . . . and she "about had a heart attack." Apparently she was a church-going woman, so when the "things" popped up and were combined with the scratches on her antique walnut table and the missing stereo components and the missing lawn chairs (which the police told her were down by the lake) and her icemaker (clogged with beer?), she'd almost had a breakdown. The financial settlement after a day's shuttle diplomacy via Willie, coupled with our promise that, really, they were leaving soon . . . this week . . . honest, was exorbitant. In the end, when we included a gift certificate to a local spa for her, the deal seemed perfectly fair and just.

By evening, Benjamin's friend Greg had arrived as well. We knew that the kids would need pals that summer to help them settle in, so we were now seven at dinner. The waitress looked at us with our three kids (tall, constantly joking, and maybe just a bit loud) and their friends (a grinning blowsy blond and an athletic-looking African American), and asked, "So, just how *many* kids do you folks have, anyway?"

Thus we began our new life in Vermont. It was early summer. The whole village smelled sweet like the blooming lilacs. We were a little more broke than we'd planned to be, and the town was just a little bit annoyed with us. We figured we'd fix that with some cheerful parties. Once they got to *know* us, it would all be different.

And it was, too. (Once they *really* got to know us they would mostly loathe us.) And, of course, we would get a whole lot more broke before it was over. But for now we played pinochle on the renovated screen porch. We drank pitchers of fresh mountain water laced with cucumbers, and I counted myself lucky and blessed to be here, with these four other people I loved, in this quiet, gently beautiful place.

That part of the story stayed true. And that is how I could tell it. We longed for new lives in a beautiful place, and nine years later we still feel glad and happy and full to be here. Or I could say we moved to a vacation spot, bought a local business where we went broke, and made a whole bunch of people mad. Neither of those begins to capture the intense beauty of this life or the exquisite mess we made for part of it. It was, and may always be, just a little bit complicated.

But look, it all turned out okay. As far as I know there are no outstanding warrants for my arrest. In this state.

Vermont.

As of right now . . . today.

≫ Chapter Three ≪

Gertrude and the Goat

After living in the country for a while, you start wanting things. Really it's no different from living in the city. You want things there, too—mostly new shoes, in my experience. Of course, what you want is shaped by what you see. If you walk down Fifth Avenue to work every day, then shoes and bags and sunglasses might make the list. If you live in the middle of the country, where the winters are long, you might crave a better lip balm and snazzier long johns.[1] You want what you see. John *thinks* he wants a pickup truck.

What I saw were chickens.

Driving to the store or to a friend's house for dinner, we would pass many farms and many houses with chickens wandering around their yards. Some of them were quite outrageously patterned, and all of them lent a sort of lovely bucolic touch to their landscapes.[2] They became an element not unlike a rock-strewn bed of flowers or a pond in the yard.

---

1. Yes, there are snazzier long johns. You'll have to trust me on this.
2. Can a person be a bucolaholic? If so, I was fast becoming one.

At the local produce farmstand, I started to ask "chicken" questions. "What kind of chicken laid that egg?" "Do they need a lot of space?" "What do you feed them?" "What's a good flock size?" Then I did what I always do in these situations —I ordered books.

Lots of books.

Before very long, I was ordering catalogs from hatcheries and mooning over various breeds, as well as the clearly yuppie water warmers with the cute little chicken-track designs on their sides. Before John could say "Absolutely not," we had a dozen day-old chicks living in our screened porch. We ordered all girls, and planned on a flock of happy lady chickens that would all take a vow of abstinence. There would be no unruly roosters to stir our girls up. Absolutely not. These were going to be friendly family pets. We gave them names like Edith and Mabel, Louise and Mildred—all "old farm lady" names. We would resist giving them each little prairie bonnets and aprons. That would have just been silly.

These lovely girls would live in the screened porch for a few weeks until the inside temperature matched an even seventy-degrees outside temperature for at least a consecutive week. This is Vermont, after all, so that ended up taking a while . . . okay, months . . . it was July before we finally got them out.

Meanwhile, I hired a local carpenter to build

our chicken house. His wife and I had split the order of chicks. Apparently, day-old chicks must be shipped in quantities of twenty-five. This is supposedly so that they will keep each other warm during the shipping ordeal. It may also be a ruse of the hatcheries to get us all buying a lot of chickens. No one seems really sure about it. At any rate, we split the order, so Matt, the carpenter, had an insight into the chicken infatuation. I had gotten a bunch of Araucanas who would, in just a few short months, be laying beautiful blue eggs in my backyard.

Matt and Val bought a bunch of fancy breeds with funny feathered heads. We were two families happily engaged in fun hippie communal chicken raising.

Matt came to our home and listened intently to my specifications. There were a few. I wanted a coop behind the house with fencing that went about twenty-four inches underground to protect our girls from foxes. I wanted lots of windows for healthy sunshine. I needed egg boxes of a certain depth for happier, more productive laying, and at least five square feet of living space for every lady. Did I mention that I had bought a few books? I also wanted a green roof and red doors. Maybe some window boxes. What? This was going to be in my yard, after all. A weathervane rooster might be nice too. Matt was . . . very patient.

As you can imagine, Matt and I were regularly visiting the local general store for materials, feed, special lights, watering troughs, and bedding . . . the usual. I chatted with Ted and all the guys there about our chicken plans. Now, these guys were Vermonters. Down-to-the-ground Vermonters. And I, most assuredly, was not. Their chickens' lives varied a bit from mine. They teased me about our "yuppie chickens," and I, perhaps not so secretly, pitied theirs. By the time Ted learned that I was laying a soft bed of pine outside the coop, he and I had grown rather tired of each other.

"You know, chickens live outside. You can't just go and change nature," with a possible "yessiree" or "nosiree"—I'd stopped listening. This was becoming a bit too much for me. We had been having these "dumb city girl" conversations for weeks now, as the chicken house went up right alongside my inflating general-store bill.

"You see, Ted, for the first few months their little feet haven't fully developed the protective skin that will keep them from getting parasites. And, you know, many chickens die from foot parasites." City girl, indeed.

"Well, now. Where'd you learn all that?" In his most sarcastic tone.

"They hide that information in books, Ted."

This kind of put a damper on the whole communal-chicken-raising party.

But pretty soon the girls were happily ensconced

in their house, enjoying soft pine and warm water. The freshest-tasting blue, almost turquoise, really, eggs were coming our way, and all was right with the chicken commune. Then, one day, we heard an outrageous sound.

We ran outside to see if something was after the flock. Foxes? Bears? Ted? To John, it looked like one of the chickens, maybe Gertrude, was making the noise. So, all the farm ladies were safe, if a little put out by the commotion. John thought that maybe, without a rooster in the flock, one of the girls had taken on a sort of lead chicken role. An alpha chicken, if you will. Complete with an attempt at crowing. Uh-huh.

Now, this was in no way your traditional *r rr rrrrr* (*cock-a-doodle-do,* for the uninitiated). It was sort of a garbled *rrr-aughhhh.* John's theory was that these were pack animals and a leader was emerging. A sort of uberhen . . .

My own theory was likewise flawed. I decided that the sound was coming from a new breed of owl we hadn't heard before. I was constantly on alert, scanning the woods, looking for this new creature. Possibly, our not seeing any owls, particularly in the morning, might have indicated a gap in the theory.

Finally we discovered the culprit. Gertrude grew a comb. The facts were too obvious, even for us, to ignore. It seemed our Gertrude wasn't a hen at all; she was a pubescent rooster whose voice was changing. The cracking *cock-a-doodle-do* was a weak precursor of the sounds to come. But yes, our Gertrude was a boy. The 0.1 percent sexing error at the hatchery had come home to roost . . . as it were. How do you tell a rooster from a hen? Apparently they hide that information in books. Books that were probably in that extensive library of ours.

Now we just had to figure out a new name . . . because things aren't always what they seem at first blush . . . or hatch.

Not long after we'd adjusted to life with Gertrude and the Ladies, Benjamin came running into the house to tell me that there was a goat . . . a *goat* . . . in our front yard. Now, we do not keep goats. We do not, chickens aside, live on a farm. But still . . . apparently, a goat. And he was right. There was actually a goat. It took a second for my eyes to take it in. Irises, hydrangeas, goat. It was a big fat billy goat with a cute little black beard and chubby horns. In the city, we mostly just got stray cats. Never a goat. I'm sure I'd remember a goat. Benjamin looked at me and asked, "So what do you do about this?"

I guessed you should maybe catch it, feed it apples, and put it in the yard, for starters. Then you call the local cheesemakers and ask if anyone is missing a goat with a blue "Number 37" tag.

"Hi there, are you missing a goat? I mean, 'Hi,

my name's Ellen' and do you know where your goats are? I'm the new neighbor, by the way. Goat. Yard. I mean, are you missing your Number Thirty-Seven goat?"

Then, while calling around and feeling pretty competent and farmworthy, you hear the goat mewing loudly and see your brand-new and very hip yuppie chickens running wildly. Just as you get to the window, you see the goat effortlessly leap over the fence, just like in that Rudolph cartoon. Of course, Rudolph was tender and sweet and filled with the holiday spirit. This goat did not have a jolly vibe. He had an agenda.

"So what do you do about this?" . . . okay. Well, what you do about this is that you feel decidedly less competent about the whole situation, as you watch the goat run away down your driveway and then down the hard road leading away from that driveway. Of course, at this point, because I'd already made a few calls, people all over town would know that the mystery Rudolph goat was in my care. They would be expecting me to be able to manage it for an hour or so, at least, until the owner could be found. I mean, it's just one goat. Of course I could manage one goat for an hour, right? Otherwise they would be required by Vermont law to talk about it for the next several mornings at the country store. This is what comes of living in a tiny community . . . this . . . *I* . . . would be news.

Plus, in some moral sense, I was now responsible for the goat. The ethics of goat-herding had never been something I was formally educated in, but you pick these things up as they happen. So, since he was running down Kent Hill toward Route 30, so was I. Did I mention that I was in my swimming suit? I was—don't ask. Did I also mention that this swimming suit was not a particularly attractive thing? This was not the kind of swimsuit wearing you might see in a Nordstrom catalog. This was the kind of swimsuit wearing you would more likely see in a health-aids catalog, with a lady in a rubber bathing cap climbing into a whirlpool. A catalog selling whirlpools . . . or bathing caps . . . rather than swimsuits. This was not my "socializing" swimsuit. And yet, running goats wait for no wardrobe.

Off we ran down the long hill, with me calling, "Here, Goat! Heeeere, Goat!" and him running . . . much faster than me, as it happens. He ran right into the middle of the only road we have that passes for busy—Route 30. Even in Vermont, this doesn't happen every day. Cars came to a stop to assess the situation.

An older man in jeans and work boots got out of his vehicle and headed toward the goat to help contain him. The goat, of course, immediately turned tail and ran right back to me—his brand-new lifelong buddy. The man looked at me standing there barefoot, in just my swimming suit, in the middle of Route 30, stopping traffic from both directions, now reunited with my friend the goat. He considered the situation for a moment, and his resulting look said that I must be a pretty poor goat keeper, yessiree.

Hunched over and holding tightly to "my" goat's collar, I trudged back up the hill. I found an old dog leash and took the goat into my kitchen—Okay, well, yes, I took him into my kitchen, because I couldn't really tie him up using such a short leash with my knot-tying skills, and clearly the chickens weren't very good goat keepers either. I resumed calling the neighbors.

Turns out that Angela at Consider Bardwell Farm had lent two of her goats to someone who was clearing a pasture. And, yes, as it turns out, Number 37, Zeus, was one of those goats. Zeus. Nice. A Greek god of a goat. She had called the pasture owner about the goats, but he hadn't called her back yet. Presumably, he was praying for a miracle and combing the local woods for the runaway Olympian. Angela allowed that, yes, she'd be around to pick up her goat in no time. Zeus and I went out into the yard to eat more apples and wait for his ride.

Just then, John pulled into the driveway. He had been out of town that morning and was just getting back. Good. Goat-sitting is probably a two-person job. John sat in the car, staring at me and then at the goat. Presumably he was remembering all the talk around the time we'd gotten chickens. Talk that might have included me wanting a cow—just one and just a little one at that, or maybe some goats. And he seemed to ultimately decide that just staying in the car was best. He figured that I had waited for him to leave town and had finally bought a goat, and he, by God, didn't want a goat. Eventually, after much face rubbing, he felt brave enough to get out and investigate.

"Ellen, why are you holding a goat in a bathing suit?"

"His name is Zeus," I introduced him, "and he's not in a bathing suit. I'm in the bathing suit, but he's in a temper. Also, he's not our goat. He's just here temporarily."

"Oh. Okay. So, he's just our temporary goat." John seemed relieved to find out that this wasn't a permanent addition to the place.

But since he did, in fact, get out of the car, I'm thinking that maybe he's coming around to the idea of a cow—just a little one—or maybe a couple of very small goats. You know, I bet he'd go for some sheep.

≫ Chapter Four ≪

Peltier's

April is polka-dotted in Vermont. The mountains are just touched with wee green buds, and from a distance it looks like a million pale-green polka dots. The occasional tree leafing out makes for bigger dots across the sides of these mountains.

Some of the sweetest bits about a Vermont spring are the sweet fresh greens climbing back up the mountains. In the autumn, we have all that bawdy red and orange rolling down at us. But the end of April is . . . almost . . . a secret. It comes blessedly on the heels of mud season, when all of the deep snow melts and turns the recently quiet rivers into raging cascades. The frozen lakes have finally given way, and right alongside all that wild beauty are muddy hillsides, choppy roads with deep rivulets of leftover river working its way onto every slope and into every yard.

Vermont is the Green Mountain State, and the end of April sees the dozens of shades of green begin to climb gently up the hillsides toward the sun. It is still chilly here, and the leaves take their time. They are buds for several days, and then suddenly the new leaf emerges.

The spring sunlight is fresh and powerful. Stand

in a puddle of it and you can feel its warmth spread across your cheeks. The sunlight is a special color for about four weeks. It's a bright pale yellow, glancing off the white clapboard houses. Those houses have been standing here, somewhat crookedly, since the eighteenth century. That spring sunlight bounces from house to house, dipping the village in a pale glow. We get a little giddy in April. The light. The polka dots. Winter is forgotten as we clean up and skip through the days touched by springtime in this beautiful place.

Living in Vermont was like being on vacation. We spent the first week moving in, of course, hanging the paintings and filling the bookshelves. Our space is very important to me, so those days were long. We would be hammering and unpacking until deep into the night, and at the first sign of the sun we would be making the coffee and getting right back to it. Friends said that it looked like we had lived here for years after only a month. Well, yes. That was actually the point.

But then came the vacation. We found a river just a short woodsy walk from home. We also discovered the Peace Street branch of the Mettowee nearby. Our dogs could roam while Eli tossed rocks and caught tadpoles. Benjamin would sketch. It was a classic babbling brook in a little piney wood, and the smell of all that summer pine was intoxicating. We would take books and a quilt . . . maybe some bread and cheese . . . and hours would pass just like a day at the beach. Hannah and I spent lazy afternoons that summer painting our toenails and reading magazines on the balcony that looked out over the Taconic Ridge. Just like we'd imagined all along. It was a heady and glorious time for our family.

Our home had been a summerhouse for years, with only occasional weekend habitation. So the local wildlife was not used to competing for the space. Raccoons played in the dead tree out back, which we nicknamed the ghost-eye tree after a favorite children's book, and the fantastic shadows it created in the early-evening twilight. Several arborists and landscape guys offered to remove it for us, but we thought it was a gorgeous, natural sculpture. I planned to plant irises around it.

There were possums and foxes, and a woodchuck who waddled through "our" yard like he owned the place. Our little piece of paper filed down at the town hall meant nothing to him, and he growled at our dogs, who were sitting in rapt attention and a good deal of bewilderment on the porch, wondering just what these things were and where in God's name they were living now. I think they missed the take-out containers in the alley back in the city.

Every day at around four or five, we would

wander down to the village and step into the cool, dark interior of the country store, where we would muse over what was for dinner. One of those days, when the store was out of the strawberries that had been in all the farmer's markets, Jay, the shop owner, told us about Pillemer's, a farmstand in Pawlet, just a short drive away.

The ride from Dorset to Pawlet only takes about ten minutes. But they are some of the most beautiful you will ever spend in a car. This is not the drama of Carmel, or anyway, not only that. Neither is it the subtler, quieter beauty of the Cape. It is, rather, an old beauty filled with stories. There are old dairies with new goats and hippie cheesemakers tending the land. There are fields of cows right out of the best kind of American photography. And, of course, there are the mountains.

Vermont has these gentle, round, green high hills that we call mountains. They wrap us snugly, like a warm quilt and a cup of hot buttered rum. Pawlet also has some craggier, more dramatic peaks. And the fields are filled with dandelions in the spring, because practically nobody uses pesticides up here. In the springtime they are fields of the happy yellow of childhood. On any summer evening, the flats, as the wide fields between the mountains are called, are filled with deer nibbling at the farmers' produce. You can see whole herds on your evening drive. There are foxes and owls and critters of all sizes that come down to these fields to feed. The farmers don't seem to mind too much. At any rate, they don't do anything that I can see to stop this natural daily feast.

We drove into Pawlet and didn't see any sign that said "Pillemer." So we kept going. Pretty soon we were thinking of turning back, and then we spotted the sheep up ahead on the pasture alongside a rolling hill. We wanted a better view. There was a river, and a hill behind it that was dotted with mama and baby sheep. The scene was so lovely and so quiet that I felt sort of like I was in a church. The sheep were grazing, walking slowly around, and baa baaa baaing like in a fairy tale. As we got back into our car, we saw the Pillemer sign just across the road.

The stand was in a big red barn next to a coop of friendly hens. We walked inside and our mouths gaped at the freshly picked produce spilling out of baskets. It was a still life waiting for the painter. This little place would have made Whole Foods blush. The owners were a married couple. He'd been an oncology doc who chucked it all for his version of a new life. They had five children with them that day, and I learned he had some grown ones besides. We bought pounds and pounds of wonderful food.

Holding the baby on her hip, Wendy would weigh and bag the produce. Her husband, Eric, would come in from the fields with big over-flowing baskets. From their fields, we could make thick sauces, and tomato and basil sandwiches that would make you cry. There were end-of-spring strawberries so sweet that too many could make your teeth ache. I would cook them with slender rhubarb into an ice cream sauce that people would beg for. I invented my now-famous strawberry salsa that June.[1]

I felt a little like I had wandered onto the set of *The Waltons*, or maybe a new movie about midcentury farm life. This was an old life we had stepped into. On future visits—we of course became regulars—we'd get there and they would have asparagus and kale, broccoli and brussels sprouts with little handmade signs telling you the variety and the price. The food was lovingly displayed in old baskets on cloth-laden wooden tables next to little jelly jars filled with wildflowers. Everything was organic, and if you wanted more of something you saw, Doc Pillemer would run out into the field in his high Muck boots, bringing you back a sack of your hankering. It all looked and tasted delicious.

Back at the country store we would load up on local organic steaks to grill alongside the kale

1. Two cups strawberries. One cup cucumbers. Half cup brown sugar, then taste; add more for a sweeter salsa. A whole bunch of cilantro. And one jalapeno pepper.

corn pie or the big salad filled with radicchio and arugula fresh out of the ground from the Pillemer's. Peltier's (pronounced "Pelchers" locally) also always had a bunch of interesting pastas and truffle oil, so our suppers could be as fancy as we wished. We immediately opened a charge account there, seemingly just like most of the town had done. For the first couple of months the reality of our spending was simply shoved into a drawer and ignored. That first month's bill was huge, but we were making sandwiches for the workers who were finishing up at the house. Of course it would be high. Then the second month was high, but we reasoned that we were still stocking our pantry. We didn't move the refrigerator fully stocked. So there were bound to be some initial price spikes. We jokingly called the store our vacation snack hut.

Finally, somewhere along about the third month, after weeks of those juicy local steaks and bacon from Vermont pigs . . . and the cheesecakes that the nuns made . . . plus the ever-present hunks of local cheeses . . . faster than you might think, all of that lovely local gourmet food began to add up. More out-of-town company than we had ever previously entertained added to the bills, but we had been going to the grocery store in nearby Manchester, as well, so these bills began to make an impact.

Now, some people might have started shopping

more economically at the big regular grocery store. Others might have cut back on the steaks. Me? I wondered how many other people had bills just like ours. And I began wondering what it might be like to own that little piece of Vermont history.

I pictured John and I driving out to Pillemer's early in the morning to stock up the shelves in the store. I envisioned myself in long flowery aprons stirring the soup, and John, maybe with a beard, carrying bags of groceries for the old ladies who walked to the store every day. My dear Eloise was the store dog. And Eli was the little boy who everyone would know and love. We would be adopted by a whole town loving us as we were coming to love them. I would bake bread and Eli and I would read about Ethan Allen beside the old woodstove. We had to figure out how to make a living up here anyway, so why not this?

Selling my end of the business in St. Louis meant that I was under a noncompete agreement for a while. Practically speaking, that meant that I couldn't open up another book business right away, but that was okay by me. I could maybe run a quaint country store. Our kids would see the value of a strong work ethic right up close. I had always traveled a lot for work, and so my kids might know that I was working without ever really seeing what went into that work. This could be different.

We could prepare and sell food that would be satisfying, and that would nurture our neighbors. Maybe we would have pizza-making classes in the big old kitchen on cold winter's nights. That would be fun, right? And we could sell lobster rolls and crab cakes out front in July. There could even be a Peltier's cookbook for the tourists. After all, I knew all about books. And I was a pretty good tourist. There would be hayrides in October with big bowls of soup and apple cider. The possibilities were endless. Heck, if it worked here we could franchise Peltier's to littl e planned communities all over the United States. There could be a little slice of Vermont village life in towns all over the country.

And tourists. I understood all about tourists who loved the Vermont vibe. I would stock specialty socks made from the wool of local sheep just for them. And those funky purses that the local farm ladies made . . . those too. We could have a section of Bennington Potters stoneware, maybe, and of course we would need an area for the kids, with handmade toys and fun little books about Vermont. What could possibly go wrong?

There were a few things we didn't know, of course.

There always are. I mean, why do something if there isn't anything to learn? So, really, you could say that what we didn't know was going to be the best part.

The store had a wine room, so we would have to learn about that. Wine could be fun. Maybe we would work out a business relationship with a California winery. We could sell private-label stock, and maybe set up some sort of Wine Country tours for the summers, while they arranged autumn leaf tours in Vermont on their end.

And then there was the building, which was nearly two hundred years old but looked to be in good shape. Well, as much as we could tell from walking around and shopping there.[2]

It seemed fine. Why wouldn't it be fine? I figured we could always barter for repairs if there was a need. Everyone had accounts there, so we could work something out.

And yes, it was also true that neither of us had ever worked in retail . . . but we had shopped.[3] Some of us a bit more than others (and a bit more shoe focused than might be useful here), but still we knew (or thought we knew) all about good customer service. And really, how much different could it be from wholesale, which I'd been doing for ages now? You bring in stock and you sell it. Selling is selling, right? No, as it turned out. Retail is a whole nother animal. And buying an established store, a grocery store for the nine

2. This is no way to evaluate a two-hundred-year-old building.
3. You would not be out of line to gasp, at this point.

months out of the year when there are no tourists, when you have never so much as run a cash box at a lemonade stand, turns out, surprising to hardly anyone, not to be such a hot idea after all. Further, the locals who shopped there just wanted to buy their canned gravy and their bread and milk and not have to fool with starstruck newbies who wanted to get their reactions to the new alpaca socks. Wildly patterned socks, even so. They must have wondered what planet had sent us here to their quiet, efficient little village. Who were we? Purple and red socks. In New England. (Really, what were we thinking??)

It was also true that we were not Vermonters. This was perhaps the most damning of all truths. Sure, we lived in Vermont now, but that hardly counted. This store was a veritable institution, owned and run by Vermonters—people who had chosen lives here going back to 1817. If you'd only been here for three generations, you were still a bit suspect. True, Dorset was filled with second-home owners, but many of them had vacationed here as children and their homes went back generations. But surely nobody loved Vermont more than we did.

Okay, okay, and yes, we had no experience in the food or grocery industries. Neither of us had ever worked in a restaurant, and this store sold breakfast and lunch seven days a week. But we did love to eat. We knew all about good restaurants, and we were both accomplished home cooks. So you know . . . how hard could it be? That question might go on my tombstone, with the answer underneath.

How hard could it be? Hard.

Really fucking hard.

So we bought the Lovely Quaint Country Store.

Of course we did.

So how do you go about buying a Lovely Quaint Country Store? First you call up the current owners and tell them just how much you love their wonderful country store. You really really love it, you say. You hint that if they were ever to consider selling it, you would be interested.[4] Turns out that they had, actually, considered the possibility of selling. What do you know? That leads to the flirting stage. And before you know it, you're playing show me yours and I'll show you mine, before making a real offer for the business. There is some negotiation, which ends up landing on a number that is astonishingly large. You know, you could renovate a nineteenth-century farmhouse for that amount of money. I know, because I was. Still, this was, after all, our new life. We went to the Life Store and picked it. "Go big" became our motto.

---

4. If you listen closely, you can hear the price going up here.

In the end, they accepted the offer and invited us to their sweet little house in the village to celebrate. Van Morrison was playing on the stereo. We loved Van Morrison and took this as another in a long line of happy omens. Clearly, we were in the early stages of some sort of dementia. They had lovely paintings of the store hanging over their sideboard. That store was, after all, the heart of the village. It felt like a tradition being passed on. Champagne was poured. Toasts were made. A perfect beginning.

I was overwhelmed with tasks. So much to do. It was hard to pick a place to begin. One of my favorite stores had always been the Vermont Country Store in Weston. I loved the big old-fashioned candy counter. I loved the kitchen room with its wonderful cheeses and dips, spread out in a tasting buffet. The toy room had Mrs. Beasley dolls and Rock 'Em Sock 'Em Robots. I could linger there for hours. I would learn from them. They could be our model. Only, we would be more authentic, set in our gracious old genuine-country-store building. We would deal in wonderfully healthy gourmet foods besides. It would be perfect.

Then there was Gillingham's, in Woodstock. They had a selection of children's books with a Vermont theme and rows of handmade Vermont soaps on display next to the Bennington Potters stoneware. And that store even smelled like a country store should: old wood, mountain air wafting through open windows, furniture polish, and root beer. I wondered if you could make that smell into a scented candle. Peltier's Country Store could be our signature scent.[5] Oh my.

And now we owned our very own country store. I imagined a shelf full of spatterware for the country kitchen. I wanted some in red for myself, and of course we could also carry blue. I could just see the rows of bowls and pitchers. It would be one of the first things you would see when you came into the store.

We would need toys. But since Dorset wasn't really a tourist destination, I figured we needed toys that were good take-alongs for folks just passing through. As a mom, I wanted stuff for the local kids, too. Whiffle bats and fishing poles in May. Maple-sugaring kits in February. We would need lots of kites, and then in the winter maybe some arts and crafts projects. Oh, and in summer we could sell a lemonade-stand kit . . . and in July, sparklers! This was really going to work.

I took an inventory of the store and began making my shopping lists. Peltier's seemed to have plenty of canned gravy and bread, but was a little short on the divine accoutrements of Vermont country life. I could fix that up in a jiffy.

---

5. At least we didn't buy a candle factory too.

I found a potter who could make coffee cups with the store image on the front. There was another vendor that could make tote bags with our zip code on them in Dorset green for the Take Home Suppers we were planning for the locals. We hung picnic baskets up high for tourists who wanted to grab a Take Home Supper and eat it over by the pond. We were going to be a haven for the locals and bring in a whole new group of tourists.

But the groceries sure took up a lot of space. I mean, it almost looked like a grocery store. I barely wondered why. Never mind that. We'd just move the row of bread to the checkout row. Then we could put the toys and the kitchen stuff center stage. Oh, and the candy.

Maybe the candy row should be right in front, so people would know immediately that they had stepped back in time. That's the kind of thing you should know right away. Also, there were a few things we were having trouble finding in the real grocery stores. Pistachio paste was scarce. Thick, old balsamics were thin on the ground. So I took home the gourmet catalogs and imagined a shelf that would rival any Williams-Sonoma. And besides, I'd get it all at wholesale prices, so just think of the money we would save at home! This store was already paying for itself.

There was, however, the little problem of seasons. Tourist season.

High season in Dorset is mostly a summer affair. In the summer, folks who own second homes come to Dorset for the season. We aren't next to the ski mountains, so we miss some of that trade. The second-homeowners tend to leave in October, so leaf season was bigger in the other towns, where tourists flocked. But I figured that we could fix that. We would just need to get on those bus-tour maps that seemed to be everywhere. And besides, a lot of tourists came to Manchester already, and Manchester was only ten minutes away. We just needed the local inns to send folks to the oldest country store in America. How hard could that be?

We bought the store in early spring. Mud season. Other states have two to four seasons. Vermont has five. Winter is long and the snow is deep. So when the snow begins to melt, the ground gets soppy wet. Mudrooms get heavy use. Some years mud season begins in March, but always by the first week of April. April we are deep into the sludge. The snow melts and runs down the hillsides, puddling in the streets and on your driveway and in your mudroom. Practically everyone lives on the downhill side of something in Vermont. Or anyway, this is how it seems come the first week of April when the water runs fast and the mud, our famous Vermont mud, is everywhere.

That was, of course, the week we bought the country store.

We had a big party on the first Saturday of our tenure right after we finalized the sale. We did. We announced it in all the local papers. "Come meet the new owners at Peltier's!" We had cider and fat loaves of homemade bread with big hunks of Vermont cheddar. I wore a long, kind of orangey linen duster over a swirling silk skirt and my usual jangley jewelry. I added a purple and orange flowing scarf that practically touched my knees.

I loved this outfit.

I was so excited.

I felt beautiful and ready for our new lives to begin.

The place was packed with people who had come out to see the people who would be taking over their beloved country store. This was fantastic. A big turnout was important to really kick things off. And seeing so much interest right away was just great. Some of these people would be our neighbors and friends . . . maybe for the rest of our lives. I couldn't wait to meet them.

One nice old lady came up and introduced herself. She had on the standard Vermont uniform, khakis and sensible shoes with a blue chambray linen blouse and some version of fleece on top. No lipstick. LL Bean. She looked steady and reliable. The nice New England lady with glasses perched low on her nose gave me a long look, a sturdy handshake, and asked me, without a trace of irony, if I was giving palm readings.

"Hi, I'm Ellen, and I'm the new owner here. We're really excited about taking over the store. So glad you could come out."

"Yes, dear. I know who you are, but I was just wondering if you were doing palm readings . . . or tarot cards . . . or what?" She smiled and added that it was a "cute gimmick" before heading back for a refill on her cider.

I didn't get it.

There were lots of people to meet, though, and I didn't have long to think about it. It wasn't until a few hours later, when a nice local lady wandered over to chat, that things became . . . uncomfortably clear.

"Welcome to Dorset. You've got quite a turnout here. I was just hearing that you've got all sorts of events planned."

"Oh, yes. Something for everyone. You'll love it. We're thinking of cooking classes in the kitchen over the winter. We'd have local folks come in and teach their favorite recipes. Maybe homemade gourmet pizza . . . or pastry chefs teaching us how to bake amazing cakes. That kind of thing."

"And were you thinking of doing palm readings?" she asked earnestly.

What the . . . ?

"You are the second person to ask me about

that, actually. Why? Are psychics popular up here?"

"Oh, no," she laughed, "but I guess they might be fun for kids' parties."

I must have looked more puzzled than she expected. She was suddenly kind of squirmy and wandered away.

The fellow standing next in line supplied the answer.

"Just what are you advertising, then, with the gypsy outfit?" he asked, with all the bluff curiosity of the well-established Vermonter.

Ah.

I got it.

The jewelry. The long scarf. Ohmygod. They thought I was in costume! The gypsy lady come to town . . .

Well, shit.

One thing I knew. I was not giving up lipstick.

I. Was. Not.

By the second week, we began to wonder where all the customers were. We hadn't been in the store much in the springtime, but we figured that it couldn't be that different from the summer. Sure there weren't any tourists, but there were still a number of locals. What about them?

We started running ads in the local papers to promote our Take Home Suppers. Thursday nights we featured crab cakes with mango salsa.

Mondays there was an ever-changing array of pasta: proscuitto and peas, asparagus and nutmeg. What fun. We didn't have to make supper twice. We'd just trundle home whatever we'd made at the store.

Strangely, we weren't selling very many of these suppers. We figured folks just weren't used to us yet. We certainly got that part right.

I was at the bank talking to the branch manager, a friendly local guy named Andy. "I've been hearing lots of news about the store, Ellen."

I beamed. I figured he'd heard about our tasty suppers . . . or maybe the rows of pottery. We'd just found a Vermont sock maker and bought three thousand dollars' worth of colorfully patterned socks. Local socks, mind you. The place was gleaming like it hadn't in years.

But that wasn't what Andy wanted to talk about. He leaned in and asked, "How's the bread?"

"The bread?" I asked, a bit uncertainly.

"Yes, the bread. I heard that you moved it."

I didn't know what to say. Sure we had moved it. Of course we had moved it. But, you know . . . so?

Then he mentioned the local high school baseball season, or something equally tangential, and we talked about that for a bit. I was glad for the change in subject. Pretty soon he asked how business was. This, at least, was something I understood and could talk about.

"Well, Andy, business is a little down from last year, but that was to be expected. We knew that would happen coming in." I was confident and enthusiastic. "We're brand-new, after all. Plus, mud season is always slow. Everyone says so. As soon as all of our new stock is on the shelves, I'm sure things will really begin to hop."

Andy seemed to be really interested in what we were doing, so I went on.

"And we just got the cutest chalkboard for out front. It's one of those sandwich boards. You know, front and back?" I may have mimed the sandwich board . . . just to make sure he understood. "Now we can show the supper menu every morning, so when folks drive by they can plan for the evening. I'm thinking on baseball game days we'll have baseball suppers. Maybe we'll offer 10 percent off to the baseball families. One of our employees is very artistic. You should see the darling little crabs she draws for the crab cakes!"

Andy seemed to want to say something, so I gave him a moment.

"But, um . . . the bread . . . ?"

Okay, so now we were back to the bread.

What? This meandering way of talking about one thing and then another until you get to the point was very New England. And I was trying. Really, I was. But, come on. The bread . . . ?

With a bit of prodding, Andy finally gave up the story. Slowly. With lots of pauses.

Apparently, he'd heard that some of the local ladies were unhappy that we'd moved the bread to the checkout.

Okay, so yes, I remembered a couple of folks asking me not "where" the bread was, but "why" we had moved it. That had struck me as a little odd, but really . . . it's just bread. It was here. Now it's over there. I figured that when they bought *their* country store, they could put the bread wherever they wanted, too. I had run a successful book wholesaling company, and I thought I just might know a little more than they did about sales.

Then I had promptly forgotten all about it.

Only, Andy, the very sweet banker,[6] . . . he wondered, in the nicest possible way, if "You think folks might have stopped coming in on account of the bread?"

His face was all scrunched up when he said it, and it looked like he might have sat in something wet. It obviously pained him a great deal to spell out his concern. But I still didn't quite get it.

People stopped coming in over the bread? Was he kidding? Was this Vermont humor? Were these people actually crazy? Or, more likely, was I just misunderstanding him?

---

6. The banker who, it must be said, worked for the bank that held the loan on the store.

I finally went for the direct approach. "Look. Please, just tell me exactly what you mean, Andy."

His face might stick this way if he kept scrunching. But finally he got it out. "Ellen . . . I hate to say it but I think what you have here . . . is a bread boycott."

Bread.

Boycott.

Only, it wasn't just bread, of course. The locals had stopped coming in at all. The bread was the reason, but the effect was across the board. Our sales were down because of bread placement.

And not only were they not coming in . . . they were talking about it. With everyone.

People were gossiping to my banker about my bread. My non-gossipy, very-uncomfortable-with-the-situation banker. Think of all the other people who must be in the gossip loop if Andy was included.

Oh. My. God.

A thought dawned: I might be in trouble here. And it probably wasn't just the bread.

❯❯ Chapter Five ❮❮

Bats and Bears
and Skunks.
Oh My.

Moving from the city to the country, no matter how long the dream has been conjured, involves a certain amount of transition shock. This goes both ways, of course. The locals are shocked all over again (no matter how many times they've seen it before) at the stupidity, the sheer witlessness, of people who have managed to live forty years or more, and presumably have held down respectable jobs, sometimes earning quite nice livings along the way. They must wonder how these people, shrieking at the sight of a wee little bat and occasionally hurling whole mattresses (called newly into service as a flying rodent trap, complete with one-thousand-threadcount sheeting) out second-floor windows, have managed to survive anywhere. And the recent transplants, likewise, wonder how civilization has failed to take root this close to real life, in this place where cell phones don't work, streetlights are an unknown, and bears eat at your bird feeders.

When we first moved to Vermont we were

warned to tag Eloise, our big Bernese Mountain Dog. From the back of her 110-pound frame, Eloise looks remarkably like a bear. The local general store guys met her and advised orange scarves for her tail and neck. It turns out that most of the bear hunters are first timers. Vermont has a lottery for bear-hunting licenses, and only a limited number are issued each year. Lots of people apply, and a man might go his whole life without ever winning the opportunity.

Bear-hunter inexperience seems to feed the local economy as well, so folks are glad to see it. First-time hunters sometimes get their bear, but in the excitement of planning the hunt hadn't given much thought to how they were going to get that four hundred pounds of Smoky out of the woods. The enterprising locals drive in with winches and tractor trailers, charging a fortune for helping the hapless hunter carry out his prize. Of course, other times these same hunters mistake big black dogs for big black bears. The newspapers all carry at least one such sad story per season. Since we walk in the woods with our dogs most days, we bought the scarves.

I had wondered how anybody ever got a bear. We were always in the woods and had never seen one. Oh, we saw their winter caves. And occasionally our bird feeders got mangled, which everyone blamed on bears. But bears themselves were illusory. Until they weren't anymore.

I was driving along Route 30 when a big black roly-poly thing lumbered across the road ahead of me. "That's a bear!" I thought. Wow, oh a bear! I was so excited I started looking for a place to pull over for a better look. I realized the bear had wandered through some thin woods that empty onto a campground where RVs park and plug in for the night. I raced into that lot and saw a man with a tiny little dog, wandering around munching on a hot dog. The wood with the bear was a few feet behind him. I pulled over and rolled down my window, suggesting he pick up his dog.

"I got it at the stand around the corner," he shouted, figuring I was asking after his lunch.

I yelled a little louder. "There's a BEAR. Bring in your DOG."

"Yeah, it's pretty good."

Oh good grief.

I got out of my car and walked closer. "Look, sir, I just saw a bear back on the road and your little dog is right in her way."

He scooped that little pup right up and glared at me with wild eyes, backing away in a fright . . . overreacting a bit, I thought. Of course, he didn't know me, but he had to know that these were the Vermont woods. These things happened. And here I was taking the time—going out of my way, in fact—to warn him, so that nobody got hurt.

Only then, a man walked slowly out of the door

of his camper and said, "Uh. No, ma'am, she's right behind *you*."

What?

Oh.

I turned around, and some four or five feet away was a beautiful three- or four- or nine-hundred-pound black bear. There wasn't a scale handy, and it seemed rude to ask her. We looked at each other for a moment, and then she slowly turned around, heading off to the bigger woods.

At least I hadn't called 911.

I have a friend who moved here to the mountains of Vermont just a few short weeks ahead of us. She warned me about calling the police. Her husband was selling their family home and closing his office, readying it for the move north, while she and the kids settled into the new house. She had fallen in love with the postcard villages, the woodsy hikes, and the idea of raising kids and dogs in such a natural setting, far away from the concrete, lights, and sirens. Unfortunately, with the nature, the quiet, and the dark there came a little wildlife.

When the first bat flew around her living room, she called 911 . . . the Vermonter who took the call was not amused. He suggested she call the "Batline" instead. Trish thought it must be like some sort of wildlife-rescue service. She tried, in vain, to find such a number in her directory. And by dialing 411. "Hello, Information, I need the Batline, please."

Eventually she trapped the scared little creature in the second-floor guest bed. Not the bed*room*. In the bed itself. She hauled the mattress (bedding and all) to a balcony door where she promptly threw it to the ground. Feeling triumphant, she expected to see the bat fly right out. When it didn't, she began to worry it would suffocate in the bedding. Because, while capturing the creature in a seventy-pound mattress and flinging it off the second floor was self-defense, letting it choke to death on Egyptian cotton seemed cruel. Come on, doesn't it?

So, using a long-handled mop, she went out and stirred the covers around, only to find that the bat had escaped.

Back into the house.

It flew lazily around the living room once again. After a bit more bat wrangling, Trish managed to trap it in a, mostly unpacked, closet. She did what anyone would do at this stage. She called 911 for the second time.

This time the guy routed her to the local volunteer fire chief. The chief, naturally, called his youngest crewmember and, no doubt giggling, sent him on the call.

Tim, a quiet, capable Vermonter, showed up and gruffly asked where the bat was. Trish, a gracious host even in a crisis, offered him tea or coffee, chatting madly as he silently went where she directed. When he opened the closet door, the bat flew right out. At Tim's face. Tim made a mad grab for it before it got airborne. The bat, as you can imagine, got away, but into Tim's hands fell a bag. This particular bag was filled with gag gifts Trish was planning to wrap for an upcoming party in the city . . . a bachelorette party. Tim tried to shove the bag back into the closet and follow the bat back into the main part of the house, but somehow he got tangled up in the blankets and clothes that had tumbled out when he'd opened the door. Tim the junior volunteer firefighter lost the battle with soft furnishings and fell back-ward, still holding the bag, which promptly spilled onto the floor.

Trish stopped screaming over the bat and looked down at a pair of licorice-laced panties resting daintily on Tim's knee. Now, that is not just something you see every day. Finally he looked up, smiled, and said, "Hi. My name's Tim." Presumably, if you're going to return someone's licorice-laced panties (or, really, any lingerie) you should at least be formally introduced.

This amusing little anecdote should have warned us all off. Certainly I would never call 911 over something as ridiculous as a bat. Nosiree, not me.

I was apparently planning to wait for a cow.

In my defense, it was a bunch of cows, and I

was driving very far, and running late for an appointment . . . a manicure appointment, but still.

So there I was on a picturesque shortcut to Rutland. The back roads were winding through the mountains. A pretty little river meandered along beside the road, and I was glad to have found this beautiful drive. I planned to only ever take this route and never the main roads from here on, because I had moved to Vermont for a reason, by God. I was here to enjoy the beauty and to enrich my soul. So, no highways for me. Only, on this particular Monday, it was raining . . . and muddy . . . and the road was slow going.

I was squinting through the windshield drizzle when I saw up ahead that something was blocking the road. Slowing down, I tried to make out what it was, until, eventually, I was breaking hard to avoid the eight or nine cows smack in the middle of my very pretty road. If you're not from Vermont, you may not have a clear picture of what I mean by "road." This was a two-lane affair, and, on the curves, "two lane" might be a bit of a generous description. Really more a lane and a prayer that the oncoming vehicle is a motorcycle. There was no going around these big girls, with the river on one side and the tree line on the other. The road itself had become a messy bunch of ruts, so turning around didn't seem likely, either.

What to do?

Okay, okay, I called 911.

I mean, the road was blocked, right? Isn't that like when a car rolls off into a ditch, and you alert the police? Or when there is a guy with a blown-out tire blocking the road? Or . . . you get the idea. Only, I didn't have very good cell service. Really it was a miracle I got through at all. And so there I was, on a rainy road, trying to make myself understood through the crackles. "Yes, I'd like to report cows on the road."

"I'm sor— ma'am, yo— br— up, could you repe— that?"

"Yes. There. Are. Cows. On. The. Road."

"Bre— up, ma'am. Bad conn—tion." And as the officer's voice broke up, I did what any reasonable person would in the situation. I made up for the bad connection by repeating myself, slower. And louder. Apparently I thought that I could fix the connection with enthusiasm.

So, yes, pretty soon I was screaming at the 911 officer that "THERE! ARE! COWS! ON! THE! ROAD!"

Oddly enough, in that way that an entire room can hush just as you say the least appropriate thing, it seemed to work. His answer came through loud and clear. "If I was you I think I'd tell 'em to move."

"Yes, thanks. I'll do that."

I'll leave you to imagine the rest. Picture me

110

getting out, in some pathetic shiny city shoes (this was before my conversion to boots), slogging through knee-deep mud, and saying "Shoo! Shoo girl!" to a fifteen-hundred-pound, soaking-wet cow and eight of her closest friends. There may have been extravagant hand gestures.

The cows, for their part, made a sound that did not quite sound like *moo.* I think their accent gave them away as not being from around here. It might also explain the language barrier, because they didn't seem to understand me either.

So I slipped and sloshed between cow whispering . . . or similar . . . and shuffling back to the car's heater, shivering as I waited for the girls to move on. They weren't in a hurry. So I sat shivering for a bit longer than I might have budgeted for this phase of the trip. Still, they did move. Slowly. Out of the way, and let me pass.

And it was a blissful, if shivering, wet, and muddy, escape. Until, of course, the car ran out of gas. Well, what did you expect? Those cows weren't going anywhere. Even after I "told 'em to move." And a person can't just sit in the middle of the road in her car soaking wet, shivering and covered in mud, without running the heater. And you really can't run the heater without running the engine. Besides, what if they moved off the road, and I had a shot at getting by? Running the engine just made sense. Right up to the point where the car began to cough and miss and I went slip sliding on foot up the road to a farmhouse, seeking refuge. A farmhouse where no one was home, which went a long way toward explaining why they didn't seem to know about the broken fence in their pasture and the eight to nine head of their cattle out for a rainy-day stroll.

So I let myself into the house. No one in Vermont locks their doors, so this was really more just being neighborly and not quite so much breaking and entering. That I know of. In this state. But they did have a phone, so I called John.

You can probably picture him quietly listening.

"There were cows. And mud. And my nail appointment. But the cows. And 911. And the heater. Out of gas. Farmhouse. Fence. And bring coffee." Even I am not brazen enough to make a pot of coffee in a stranger's kitchen. Armed robbery, maybe. Entering (if not breaking), sure. But unauthorized beverage preparation is right out. I've got principles.

He sweetly showed up with the coffee, and warm socks, which made me want to marry him all over again.

We did leave a note though. It said, "There is a hole in your fence and your cows are loose."

Because we are Vermonters now, and we stick to the facts.

And, yes, you would be correct in presuming that we would only call ourselves Vermonters in the presence of other newcomers . . . or outsiders. Because we've got a few generations to go before we officially earn the title from the locals. But I have to admit, the initiation process can be a bit . . . challenging.

One morning, a while after we had settled up here, we had a teensy little hint of a skunk problem. Give me bats and bears any day, but God save us from skunks.

So, every morning we get up and let the chickens out of their house. It's a nice house, but they like to spend some time in the yard and at our kitchen window. At night, however, we like to keep them as safe as possible from the predators.

John had just come back in from letting the chickens out when we heard a terrible ruckus. Yes, a ruckus. That's the official term for a loud problem in your chicken house. It's in the books. In our library. Trust me.

My farmer-husband ran back outside to see a skunk sauntering off with a chicken firmly in tow. So, as any well-established transplanted midwesterner with a New England chicken house, he hollered at the skunk. He threw rocks. The skunk sauntered right past him and grabbed a second course on his way through. Well, shit.

Eli, a bit of an outdoorsy wild child, grabbed his BB gun and went to the defense of the homestead. A Green Mountain BB Boy. John herded the flock back into the chicken house, as

Eli peppered the thief with BBs. As you might imagine, the skunk didn't care for the BBs, so he charged Eli and started spraying.

Eli quickly got out of the way and was, thank goodness, not hit by the spray. Between the rocks and the BBs, the skunk decided that this was no kind of yard for him and left. The yard was pretty stinky, of course, but there was a nice wind blowing, so the cloud didn't stay long.

A rough morning that cost us two of our hens, but in the end it could have been much worse. I know this because in the afternoon the skunk came back. And it *was* much worse.

Apparently, the varmint thought that chicken breakfast was such a success that he'd give chicken lunch a try. It had been hours, really, so I had let the dogs out, figuring that he was long gone. But who am I to figure about such things? What do I know about skunks? Chickens, yes . . . I did the reading, but skunks . . . not so much.

We first knew something was going on when we heard the dogs barking like mad. They had cornered the creature way down in the backyard. By this stage we had added to the pack, and these pups had all grown up with hens in the yard. They were very protective of their chickens. I'm probably not giving away too much here to mention that skunks really don't like being cornered. I suppose we all know about this, but the dogs were . . . well, being dogs. And apparently they didn't know. We'd never told them.

Oscar, a Wheaten Terrier, ran . . . bravely, I guess . . . through the noxious skunk fog and grabbed the critter in his mouth. He pinned it down with one paw, as Violet, our Bernese pup, barked like crazy, and Pippi, a Moodle, attacked from the rear. There may have been more noise coming from the humans in the equation, who were yelling at Oscar to drop that creature. Which he did. Good Oscar.

Of course, then the skunk meandered . . . confidently strolled, even . . . across the yard, spraying, well, pretty much everything. The dogs chased him in a giant circle, succeeding mostly in fouling even more of the yard than the skunk could have hoped to hit. John, quiet, contemplative, writer John, yelled, in the loudest, meanest voice I have ever heard come out of him, for the dogs to *"COME!!!!!"*

That, naturally, meant that he sharply inhaled right after yelling, and in the process sucked down a quart or two of the skunk spray. The yell worked, though, and the dogs gathered round as we ran into the house. Did I mention that the dogs were young? And excitable? Because they were. And in their excitement they ran absolutely everywhere in the house. Every. Square. Inch.

Now, you might be thinking that skunk smell is unpleasant—we've all smelled it on the highway as we passed through an unpleasant spot or two—but I can tell you that a skunk attack, up close, is on a whole different scale. We seemed to be frying rotten eggs on a flaming old tire. This smell passed unpleasant long ago on its way to terrifying and had finally landed pretty firmly in the land of god-awful.

As we assessed the damage, we thought that Pippi had taken the worst hit. She smelled so bad, in fact, that we didn't realize that Oscar and Violet were drenched in the spray. Our noses had been so corrupted that it seemed like it had only hit Pippi . . . that was a relief . . . if a nonsensical one, until it wasn't. Our house was ground zero of a thermonuclear skunk bomb.

I was slack-jawed and stunned. And my eyes were watering.

John puked.

So here we were. Fouled beyond reason. Vomiting. Made prisoners in our house by a varmint that Eli's BB gun had only transformed into a snarling, spraying hell-beast, with our three reeking, barking dogs, two dead chickens, and a henhouse full of terrified poultry. What the hell to do, right? We considered calling the game warden. But the game warden around here would take at least a day or two to come. He might have the number of a trapper, but there are hardly any people around here. So the trapper might have to come from New York. How long could that take?

Meanwhile, we were standing on the screened porch watching the skunk at the back of the meadow tucking into the chicken formerly known as Edith.

We could call 911. And, no . . . just, no. This was not a story I wanted to hear about for the next few years. Besides, who knew if Tim, the volunteer firefighter, would even be on duty.

So, in the spirit of reasoned, well-intentioned wildlife conservation and to some extent pacifism, I called Benjamin, my oldest . . . the hunter . . . and told him to "Bring your shotgun." This is not a phrase that I had ever imagined myself turning when I lived in St. Louis.

Of course, he came. How often is his mom really going to ask him to shoot something? He bounded out of his car, gun in hand, ready to do his bit. Only to find that he had, in his hurry, forgotten to bring any shells. Well, of course he did.

"No shells?"

"Nope. I was in a hurry. You said to hurry. I guess I could go get some."

"You're sure you don't have any in the car?" I asked, knowing my son.

And there was, in fact, one lonely shotgun shell rolling around in his glove box. He'd forgotten about it as well. He stood up, proud of his find, and announced, "Don't worry, Mom, it'll only take one."

Off he strode into the yard with one shell. And yep, there the little bastard of a skunk sat lunching on poor Edith. Benjamin raised the shotgun, took aim, and sure enough, one shell, one shot, one dead skunk.

Apparently we're farmers now. I have a new appreciation for guns. John thinks maybe we should vote Republican in the next election. I assured him that was skunk spray talking.

So, in not our best state, we went to the pet store and loaded up on "skunk stuff." The staff told us that this had been their third skunk sale in two days. The weather had, apparently, triggered a "store up for winter" instinct in the skunk population. Who knew?

We soaked the dogs in the stuff. Three separate times, actually. But really, who's counting? We scrubbed ourselves clean, too, but apparently we had inhaled far too much of the skunk bomb. You might ask, "How much is too much?" Turns out, you know it's too much when the whole house has a sore throat and nausea. And as soon as we had the human vomiting under control, the dogs decided that they really hated to be left out of the fun, so they joined in as well. All. Night. Long.

When I was finally mostly clean and able to process the whole situation, I decided to take some table scraps out to the poor chickens. I mean, they had lost two of their sisters and been assaulted by varmint and people alike. It hadn't been a good day for them. They deserved a treat. So out I went with potatoes and corn in hand.

A funny thing about chickens, when they are frightened they will hide in the rafters.

Having diarrhea.

On my head.

Vermont is a beautiful place. A land of natural beauty. Beauty that will, on occasion, fling lingerie at nice young men, run your car out of gas on a lonely road, terrify the dickens out of campers, and shit on your head when you bring it a treat.

I'm sure this wasn't in the Disney-movie version of New England that I'd signed up for.

➤➤ Chapter Six ◀◀

Arrested Again[1]

Parent-teacher conferences were back to not being fun since the move.

Now, we are the kind of people who believed in public education. Still do. But we had three kids all with very different and distinct educational profiles. Our oldest, Benjamin, had been the one who broke us in. He is a brilliant, six foot four, sweet lug of a guy with the attention span of . . . a mature flea. His is the picture they show next to the abbreviation "ADHD" in the dictionary. He had always been really big for his age and simultaneously young for it besides. Picture the gentle nine-year-old giant at the ice rink who comes off the ice and unlaces his skates for a little break to get new gloves from the car. Only then he notices the humongous ice hill that the Zamboni has made, so he grabs his skateboard instead. Of course, he forgets the gloves and naturally leaves the car door wide open. He is on the hill and rolling down it forty-five seconds before I can get to him. That time, his ankles and wrists held.

---

1. Well . . . almost.

But many bones had been broken from just those kinds of impulsive moments.

Benjamin sat practically upside-down in every chair, with his head nearer the ground than his feet. He was on the All Drumming Channel, all the time. Every table. Every seat. Every flat surface. Drums, one and all. When you walked behind my son in a department store you watched things fall off every rack he walked near. The kid left a wake.

So, you know, I was the mom who worked for every bond issue in our public school district so that we could have a hope of requesting the sweetest, gentlest, kindest, most excellent teachers they had. Plus, I volunteered in his classrooms regularly. But it was not enough.

The classes were too big, and the teachers were stretched too thin. The year Benjamin's sixth-grade teacher, the one I had handpicked, upended a desk in the middle of the room as an example of how she handled messy desks, we knew we were at the end of that particular road.

I told him that he didn't have to go back. A mad scramble of school visits and interviews ensued. Of course, eventually we found one. A perfect one. One where there were about ten kids in a class. The classes had lofts and couches and the teachers understood kids like my boy who needed to move his body in order to learn. Eli was still just a baby, but they also understood our girl, Hannah. She's the natural-born academic. She was the kind of kid you could put in a closet with a flashlight and a book and she would learn to read it. Here, though, with ten kids in a class, there was room for every kind of learner. Everyone could get tended and challenged. The price tag for a move like this one was high. Nothing in our backgrounds had prepared us for this. But I had just gotten my first good commission check and our kid was struggling. We figured one year at this school was better than none. We'd take it year by year and figure it out as we went.

And we did. For years we sent the kids to that wonderful little place we'd found back when Benjamin was just eleven. New City School, where teacher conferences were a joy. Seriously. We always enjoyed them. New City had no report cards, with what had always seemed like silly subjective grades. They didn't use timed tests, which might have been designed to trick kids into scoring poorly. New City understood that that was not where real learning happened.

New City was built around Gardner's theory of multiple intelligences. So it focused on helping each student develop in the ways most important to their particular intelligence. A spatial learner? Maybe in your English class you'd like to draw a map with all of the places where the characters learned lessons, and then draw pictures that illustrated what those lessons had been. A logical, mathematical type? Then, you might create a game designed to teach the grammar lessons you found in the story. Maybe math class is tough for you, but you're a musical type, like Benjamin. Then perhaps Mark, your brilliant, loving math teacher, would work on algebra with you on a djembe. Your drumming skills could shine, and the math would come along for the ride. A well-organized linguistic learner like Hannah? Then maybe you could teach a class on bread making. The eleven-year-old boys apparently needed a lot of help. Hannah wondered how they could be so helpless at bread making and still grow up to be president. Bread-making feminism, I suppose.

New City had been magic, and I admit that we were spoiled.

Only, now we were more than a thousand miles away from our beloved New City, and our little local public school was just not working for Eli, according to our parent-teacher conference. His teacher spent our conference telling us about his "zingers." Eli's zingers were, apparently, the ironic comments that John thought all the time, but which Eli actually said. Out loud. In class. Zingers.

Oh, and there was also the roof. Apparently, Eli had figured out how to climb up on the roof of the school. He was climbing up there to get errant balls . . . or Frisbees . . . So, using his powers for good, but still, he was seven and on the roof. The teacher, perhaps unsurprisingly, didn't like it.

So I decided that I should probably talk to Eli about the whole thing. I figured I should at least find out what was going on from his perspective.

"Honey," I said, "your teacher mentioned that you say things during reading time. Things like 'Where's that Snickers when you need it?' while other kids are reading. That doesn't seem polite. Honey. How come?"

Eli quickly responded that "It's soooo boring. We take turns reading out loud, and it takes so loooong."

"But, hon, the child who's reading doesn't want to know you are so bored you are dying for a Snickers." Eli is a considerate kid. He'd understand.

"Mo-om! Noooooo. The guy *in the book* was in a plane crash and he was starving. *Actually starving*. All. Week. Long. We just could not get him out of the woods, where he was so hungry. I figured he needed a Snickers in his pocket. I needed one, too. And everybody laughed, including the kid who was reading." So that explained a few things.

Second grade. I knew we were in trouble. It is a short hop from bored to trouble when you are a seven-year-old boy.

When we moved here, we had found a great, hip mountain school, the Long Trail School, for

Hannah, our seriously academic girl. It was a sixth-through-twelfth-grade school, though, so that wouldn't help us with Eli for a while. But I was politically liberal, after all. I still believed in public education. Believe. Present tense. I have always voted for every education tax or bond increase everywhere I have ever lived. And here in New England, the education capital of practically the whole world, where the villages were small and sweet, surely, I figured, the schools would be, too. Also, the other independent school was one town away, which wouldn't have been a big problem, but it was also a feeder for New England boarding schools. Boarding school was not a fit for us. Quality time over quantity time had always sounded like a big load of BS to me. I figured that you needed proximity, and lots of it, for quality time to happen. You can't just decree it.[2] We wouldn't be sending them away anytime soon.

So, we just needed to be effective advocates both for our little boy and for the local school. That, anyway, was the plan.

Eli went off to school on the Tuesday after the conference, promising to try and curb the zingers.

---

2. There are probably some folks reading this who knew our kids during their teenage years. They might tell you that plenty of people thought we'd made a big mistake.

Well, he could try, anyway. John and I headed to Pillemer's to get produce for the store. Between the beets and the carrots, I noticed the Pillemers' daughter, a pretty little thing of about eleven, loading up our baskets. I wondered why she wasn't in school.

She explained, "Oh, I'm homeschooled."

Hmmm. Having spent much of my adult life working with libraries, I'd heard of homeschooling, of course. My library wholesale company had stocked tons of homeschooling materials. Librarians were always getting requests to carry more titles for homeschoolers, so we kept quite a bit of it. But, in the Midwest, homeschooling had seemed to be mainly a religious choice. I didn't know anyone like us who had made the decision to homeschool. We had never, even briefly, considered it in St. Louis.

I peppered her with questions. I mean, this kid seemed so smart, and so happy here. And I knew that her parents were very interesting people. Smart people. Her father was an oncologist. Her mother ran this whole thriving operation. I really had to know more. So in the afternoon I came back and peppered her mom with even more questions.

"How does it work? This whole homeschooling thing?" I asked.

"Beautifully, actually," she said. "We're all very happy with it. The kids take standardized tests every spring to make sure they're where they need to be. Right now, she's three years ahead of grade level."

"What do you guys do? I mean, what's it like?"

"We do pretty much whatever we want, really."

I'm all for free form, but I wasn't sure if we'd have the right idea of how to put together a "third grade."

"Did you buy a curriculum from somewhere?" I asked.

"Just for math. We created our own curriculum for reading, writing, and history."

Wait. I still had Benjamin and Hannah's portfolios from New City. I wondered if I could model one after theirs.

"But doesn't your daughter miss the other kids? School activities? That sort of thing?"

She laughed. "With all these brothers and sisters it isn't very lonely. And besides, she joined lots of groups for music and sports. So, no, there are lots of kids in her life."

Well now. That's a lot to think about. I wonder if we could really pull it off? Would we want to? Would it be good for Eli? For us? Luckily, our son helped us decide.

Eli came trudging home that afternoon. He had gotten in trouble. Another zinger, apparently. According to Eli, the boy in the book they were reading had seen something in the sky, and he was hoping for a rescue. Eli's response had been, "It's a bird! It's a plane! It's a peanut butter and jelly sandwich! Thanks folks, we are saved!"

So, Eli, our seven-year-old second grader, was asked to write a paragraph about interrupting in class. I guess his teacher didn't like peanut butter.

So anyway, he did what he was asked. He wrote about interrupting class.

He wrote that interrupting class made it less boring.

"So, what about homeschooling?" I asked.

Everyone was intrigued. Benjamin offered that he wished we had thought all this up a lot sooner. He wondered if you could homeschool college. Hannah had a boy in her class at Long Trail, Thad, who had been homeschooled, and he was goofy, uninhibited, and the smartest boy she knew. Our research began in earnest.

As news spread, people, unaccountably, began to get irritated with us. Okay, so more irritated. But, still. We were still going to local parties, at this point. We were, even, still getting invited. It was good for the store, we reasoned, so we went. John and I have never much loved parties or been very social. That was a good thing, since as business dried up so would the party invitations. But in those early days, we went.

We knew that we would pretty quickly meet the two or three friends that we would probably keep. We tend to seek out the few people in any large group that we like, and then stick close to them. We just had to go out in the world until we found them. We figured they were unlikely to find us in our pajamas in front of the fire. So, out we went.

The cocktail hour was still alive and well in Dorset, Vermont, when we moved here. Lots of very nice people invited us over for a glass of wine and to meet their neighbors. These folks would, presumably, be our customers at the store, so we went to lots of cocktail parties. But then word got out that we were planning on home-schooling Eli the next year.

I explained to these new acquaintances that, "You know, we have always wanted to live in Italy for a year. You know, just slip away and immerse ourselves in another culture. So, homeschooling would be a good start." I figured this would be a way for them to accept our decision without attaching any criticism to it.

The rumors started flying that we were moving to Italy. So I had to be clearer. I may have mentioned that Eli was a little bored.

Bored?!

"What's wrong with our school? So, are you too good for the local school?" The outrage built in pitch and volume. I had not expected this.

I, naturally, replied that "No, no, of course we're not too good for the school. But Eli is used to smaller classes. You know, maybe eight or ten kids. And this class has twice that. So we were thinking about a change, is all." Surely they could understand that. Right?

Apparently, everyone we met had a relative who worked at the school. Our even thinking about homeschooling as a choice was an insult to just about everyone. Including, as it turns out, our trash guy. He pointed out that he had learned to read and write in that school, and now so did his kids. Did we think he was stupid? Oh boy. Not the conversations we had planned on having.

Then, of course, everyone wanted to know what our qualifications were. How were we going to teach Eli as well as the school could? And so I may have started getting a little bit snippy myself.

Were we trained in history and English and science and math? No, but then neither were the third-grade teachers at the school. They majored in something, sure . . . philosophy or anthropology or poli-sci . . . and then they taught everything. We were talking about third grade, here. I mean, you know, Davy Crockett and the Alamo . . . the Hardy Boys. How hard could it be? Sure, some teachers majored in education, which seemed to have a lot to do with classroom management. How was that beneficial for Eli? Learning to line up and be quiet? I had some opinions about being quiet. They weren't very popular opinions at the school, but I wasn't offering to rewrite their curriculum. I was just thinking of making up my own for my own kid, for goodness' sakes. It was shocking to me just how many people thought that they knew what was best for my child. These same folks who were sure that I wouldn't be able to teach my kid because I didn't have an education degree were certainly willing to offer their un-degreed opinions about how to teach him now. Come to think of it, why do these parents assume they can teach their kid how to walk and talk and swim and play and interact with other children and take care of animals and develop compassion and curiosity, but then as soon as the kid turns five they turn the whole thing over to someone else?

Suddenly the whole concept of public education seemed wrong for me. I had never liked group activities. Why had I bought into this one? What about the little souls who were smarter or slower than the rest? Who was going to help them blossom? Who was going to teach the other kids kindness and compassion and patience? Who would teach them to develop their own creativity at their own pace, unhindered by the mean, petty judgments of others? Wasn't adulthood plenty time enough to face the bastards in the world? Wouldn't a well-loved child who had been taught to think critically at his own pace be better equipped than one who had been shunned or bullied, who was regularly in trouble, or who just faded into the background? And just who was going to kindle my own child's wonderful sense of humor and irony for eight hours every day? Who better than me? Who better than someone who loved him? Whose idea was this, anyway? I may have gotten a little zealous about it all.

So of course I began creating lesson plans right away. There would be lots of writing. Kids need to learn to write. So we would read newspaper articles every day and talk about current events. Okay, so we already did that. We had politics every night for supper, but now we could do it all the time during the day when we were wide awake. This was going to be a blast.

And journaling. We could both journal. So, we'd be doing reading, writing, and critical thinking. But then there was math. The store would be good for math. Maybe we would have Eli work at the register sometimes with John, and he could learn to make change. I bet the customers would like him.

Then there was research. Kids who don't learn to research before high school are really missing out. In third grade, Eli would do three research papers. He could pick whatever he wanted to study and then we would research it together. Note cards! There could be note cards. Did they still use note cards?

I was never great at math or science, but John was. So he could teach those. Maybe not at first. At first, we could do it together. I mean, I could add and subtract, multiply and divide.

This was, after all, third grade we were talking about. But the trick was to make it fun.

In science, we could study the town pond. We could track its changes over a year and learn about the seasons and the water and the ecology of the pond. We could learn about the sustainable world around us here in Vermont, raising chickens and growing gardens that would feed us. Finally, we decided that we would pick a theme and tie every-thing into that theme. Sort of like *This American Life* on NPR. Then the pond could be part of the literature choices somehow. And we could tie the literature to a historical period and study the history that way. Maybe we could cook old recipes that Davy Crockett might have eaten from the food that we grew. Or maybe we could study Ethan Allen and compare him to our modern political leaders. Who said it all had to come in a certain order? The trick was to kindle desire and curiosity and to learn to think.

Eli was not a morning guy, so we figured that school surely didn't have to start at eight and end at three. We would be a homeschooling house. Learning could happen anytime, and we would be on alert for it. He did love to play with kids after school, though, so maybe a little late-morning work, and then an early-afternoon and evening session. Of course, without all that lining up bullshit, I figured we could pack in a whole day in about half the time of regular school. That part turned out to be right. Soon after we started homeschooling, Eli was testing way ahead of his grade level, and mostly it all managed to seem like play. Homeschooling became the great surprise of my middle years.

Eli loved pirates. He was almost eight and he loved anything that smacked of adventure. So adventure was the theme we took for third grade. During the research phase, I had talked to every smart person I knew about how to teach third grade. I called every educator I respected. Mark Norwood, the best teacher I have ever known, cast the deciding vote for us.

"What's the worst that can happen? In third grade, so long as you know how to read and write, you will be fine. You guys will probably have a bunch of fun."

That was good advice. He turned out to be so right. Homeschooling—what a blessing. It had taken the slower, more thoughtful pace of Vermont for me even to think of it.

So, we were deep into *Treasure Island* for English class. Long John Silver was made for little boys. We carved knives. We made pirate flags. We read and picked up new vocabulary words like "stockade," "buccaneer," and "cutlass." Then we got arrested.

Okay, not exactly arrested. Just nearly arrested.

We had remodeled the upstairs above Peltier's into our classroom. We'd painted and put cheerful paintings and shelves up. We got a cushy couch for snuggling up to read in front of the woodstove. I thought it was a little like *Little House on the Prairie*. Well, my version of *Little House on the Prairie*. I'm not sure they had the same kind of upholstery at the Ingalls house, but I was very happy with the setup. So was Eli. John was intermittently glad. He was glad when he was upstairs with us. Not so much when he was downstairs in the actual store.

We were even learning about chemistry in *Treasure Island*. The chemistry of homemade rum. But, chemistry. You know, science. We built a boat, too, and took it down to the pond in Dorset to see if it would float. Eli thought we needed a little war, so we had also brought along some fireworks and red food coloring for the necessary bloodbath.

The food coloring was in this giant two-gallon jug that had been in the back of the store kitchen when we'd bought the place. We could never figure out exactly what it was supposed to be for, so I imagined it could create a little blood around a shipwreck pretty neatly.

---

3. Okay, these were actually Benjamin's old army guys, but we tied little bits of cloth around their heads and were pretending they were pirates. Argh!

Happily, the boat sailed and we had a bunch of little plastic pirates[3] who were engaged in an epic battle. We'd just finished the book, and we were writing a book report about it. This trip to the pond was the celebration at the end. I'd brought along a boom box (remember those?) and had a tape of cannon fire and war sounds, which we were playing at full blast. Eli thought that the battle scene needed a little blood, so he decided to use a little of the food coloring, only it spilled.

Or anyway, that was what I told the police. I'm not sure whether or not that was precisely true. It might have been true. It also might have been that he had just dumped the whole thing in the pond.

Or it might even have been true that it was too heavy for him to dump, so I might have lifted it and, really through no fault of my own, it spilled. Or possibly I dumped it into the pond in the happy ecstasy of battle.

Whatever.

What I do know is that the red water spread and spread and spread and kept spreading. It was amazing how fast that whole pond looked like the Red Sea. This was a chemistry lesson of its very own. Eli was thrilled. I was . . . a little worried.

The lady walking across the street wandered over to see what all the cannon noise was about. At least she didn't call 911. Eli started telling her about *Treasure Island*, and she was kindly nodding her head, smiling, and listening when all of a sudden she noticed the pond. She, sort of, screamed.

"Get back from the edge! Something horrible is growing in there. Stand back! Step away! Oh my God!" Lots of exclamation marks.

Eli, very calmly, started to explain. I squeezed his hand. The neighbor ran home and . . . so did we. I'm pretty sure that this is when she called 911.

I carried the red food coloring jug straight to our Dumpster. I may have covered it with kitchen garbage, just in case. I wondered if the CSI folks could find it in there. Maybe I could get an early trash pickup that week.

Pretty soon we saw the fire engine go up the street. The state police were in on it too. Not much in the way of crime or environmental disasters happen around here. So this sort of call gets a lot of attention. Well, I guess these sorts of things didn't used to happen. Before we came to town, anyway.

Half the town seemed to be passing by the store. I watched from the window. It could be said that Eli and I were hiding. One of us was, anyway. Eli was eating his lunch. He didn't know we were on the lam.

John was at a liquor-licensing class, so I was imagining what would happen to Eli when the police inevitably came to take me away. Would he be put in foster care till someone could reach John? Cell phones didn't work very well here. How would I tell anyone what was happening? Who would pick up Hannah from school? I decided, finally, that I had to face the problem. I put Eli in the car, and we drove down to the pond. (This trip, I didn't let him steer the car. Prudence.)

"Why are the police here?" he asked. "And fire trucks? What's happening, Mommy? Why is everyone at the pond?"

"Oh, sweetie, we turned the pond red with all that damned food coloring, and I think maybe the town is worried." And probably the EPA.

"Are we in trouble?"

"You aren't, sweetie." I on the other hand might have been about to find out if the Dorset jail looked like the Mayberry jail. I wondered if Otis was sleeping it off. "Don't worry," I assured him.

Then Eli summed up the whole situation . . .

"Oh shit."

Had that been a vocab word? I didn't think so. But it was a nice little summation nonetheless.

I got out of the car and asked Eli to stay put. I went up to the policeman, who had brought all these orange cones to block access to the pond, and I began explaining.

"Hi there. See, Eli had been a little bored in second grade. He is so much like his father, and irony looks and sounds different in a seven-year-old than it does in an adult—"

"Ma'am, we have an environmental problem. Maybe a disaster. We have called the folks at UVM and you need to get back in your car right now." He was stern, concerned, and not all that interested in second grade.

"Uh-huh. Well, sir, that's what I was trying to explain. You see, we decided to homeschool our little boy and we were reading Long John Silver. That's just what we called it. It's actually *Treasure Island* and . . ." I may have been stammering. My neck was definitely all blotchy and red. I looked like a bit of an environmental disaster myself, come to think of it.

"Ma'am! Get back in your car now!" My stammering admission was not playing with this audience.

"Oh just listen to me, would you?! This is *not* an environmental disaster. Or probably not. Hell, they turn the river green in Chicago every year for St. Paddy's Day and no one ever dies from that. I mean, *I* made the pond red. It's food coloring, for God's sake!"

That slowed him down some.

He got, sort of, quiet.

And then slowly he said, "You vandalized the pond with food coloring?"

So then I explained again about *Treasure Island* and the zingers that brought us here and good old New City, and then the pirate fight and the . . . er . . . spill.

At least, I think that's what I said. It kind of all started running together about then.

Eventually I told my long story with its rambling run-on sentences to a couple of more men in uniforms. Everyone slowly went home.

It started raining while I explained. It rained enough that afternoon that the newspaper couldn't get a picture of Bloody Bay. Thank God.

I didn't have an umbrella. And at that point, I surely didn't care.

⋙ Chapter Seven ⋘

Holidays and Holy Days

We have a secret up here, but I am going to tell it to you. Winter has a smell. So does snow, actually. It really does. They are perfectly distinct from one another.

Winter smells like wood smoke, thick winey stew, bread baking, and the old burner when it is newly full of oil. Everyone believes that. Snow smells like freshly pressed linen . . . or maybe raw silk. Generally, only northerners can believe that.

Have you ever been to one of those boutique stores that specialize in linens and natural, raw fabrics? They are constantly steaming the clothes in those places. Imagine that crisp smell, in that close place, and then . . . just for a moment . . . strip away all of the warmth. That is the smell of snow. Now, toss in a little wood smoke piping out of your neighbors' chimneys, and you will have the smell that lingers just outside our back door.

At night, when the moon is full and the snow is sparkling crisp, the smell is perfectly clear. There are no warming cars. No wet, barking dogs. No kids snacking on something crunchy and wrapped in plastic. Then that smell envelopes you like the smell of clothes fresh from the dryer. It is too cold for the loamy smells of May. It is too cold even for the smell of the piney woods. At ten below, you, your hats, your mittens, and your coats are over-whelmed by the smell of snow. Really. I swear.

I know this because, during our first winter here, I drove into a snowdrift. I hit a small patch of ice and braked, uselessly, it turns out, while my car careened slowly down the sloping side of the road. I tried to back out and only succeeded in digging myself even deeper into the bank.

Luckily, I was close to home. I pushed hard and opened the car door, stepping into four feet of snow. I walked . . . trudged, really . . . all the way home. My skirt and long johns were soaked. The snow was deeper than my legs are long. I stepped into the house and the smell of snow was so powerful that it brought John calling, "Hey, somebody left a door open. The snow is coming in."

Nope. Just me. The Abominable Snow Wife, coated from the waist down and filling the house with fresh snow. I headed for the tub, while John headed out on the car-rescue mission. I sat in a deep tub full of hot water, grinning. It was the smell of snow that brought him out. Snow has a smell. Who knew?

Here's something else they don't tell you before you move to your northern, isolated, beautiful mountain paradise. Winter is loud.

Sure, first there are those silent snowfalls, and you are deeply in love. You stand amidst the tall pines watching millions of those fat flakes fall and swirl to the ground. There is so much beauty amidst so much action that the silence is amazing. Then, too, there are those bright blue days when the temperature is five below, and through all that cold sunshine you can see for miles. The air is so still and so quiet that I find myself using a word like "awesome." "Awesome" is a word that the kids use for a good pizza, but that I used to reserve for Christmas Eve and singing "Silent Night" with a baby in my arms. At first, winter is a quiet lover. And you can't get enough.

Only after you have been here for a while, and are no longer just a weekender . . . then you get the real story. Because, in between those cold weeks, there are days when the temperatures climb into the thirties. And on those days, the ice on the slate roof begins its secret melt.

Then, one evening, just as you are settling into the tub, it happens.

WHOMP![1]

WHOMP is, apparently, the sound of ice sliding off of the roof. It is not a gentle, quiet sound. Hurricanes are quieter. Windows rattle. Slate tiles fly off, of course, which is why the roofers in this part of the world all seem to live in such big,

---

1. Which is not, generally, the sound I hear when I slip into the tub.

cushy houses. The animals hide under the beds. So when you hear the WHOMP, you might be tempted to run outside to see what's happening. That might result in a sheet of ice flying off at you and narrowly missing taking your arm off. So if you were me, you might run back inside.

Shutters get hit by the falling ice and hang lopsidedly for the rest of winter. Of course, you might plan to fix them, but the day after the ice melts there is probably going to be a cold snap, an ice storm, and that would make climbing up the side of your house pretty perilous.

No one mentions the wind, either. These are windstorms that are louder than I ever experienced in tornado country. We are in a high valley surrounded on all sides by these sweet round nurturing Vermont mountains. But the nor'easters that you hear so much about on the news . . . this is their backyard. Being in the middle of these mountains is being in a wind tunnel. It whips around the house. It yawns and moans. If the temperatures are even a little variable, we get wind and ice melting at the same time and it feels a lot like your house . . . the one that you spent weeks renovating . . . the one that you owe a fortune on . . . is falling down.

So the first winter we were here, I did, well, yes, I did call 911.

"Nine-one-one, what is your emergency?"

"My roof is falling off."

"Ma'am?"

"The roof. My roof. Falling off. There was a WHOMP! And then I went outside, and then my roof tried to chop off my arm at the shoulder."

"Are you injured, ma'am?"

"Well . . . no."

But it was falling off. I mean, it was.

Huge piles of slate were piling up. I couldn't let the dogs out. We moved our cars to the bottom of the hill, and then fought our way through the snow and ice back to the house. I watched and worried as even the fire in our fireplace blew itself out. It seemed—not to be melodramatic here—a bit like the end of the world.

John was visiting Benjamin at college. Hannah and Eli and I were huddled up, and I felt unable to protect us. Then I began to fantasize about small towns and community action. I imagined all these strong Vermont firefighters (Hi, Tim) pulling up and lashing big sheets of something strong to my roof to protect my newly restored farmhouse. I figured they all must admire us for buying this old 1838 farmhouse and bringing it back to its glory, right? We weren't like those silly city people who moved here and built McMansions. We didn't put up all those ridiculous lights around our property, blotting out the stars. Nosiree. I understood living with integrity in this beautiful place.

Uh-huh.

What was I thinking? I was imagining some kind of *Little House on the Prairie* barnraising ceremony, but instead I was breathlessly offering to the 911 operator that my roof was falling off.

"Ma'am, where do you live?"

And then he asked . . . I swear I'm not making this up, "Are you the folks that brought in those foreigners to fix up your house?"

So, yeah . . . I guessed I was . . . so I said "Yes" just as another bunch of tiles crashed to the ground.

WHOMP! WHOMP!

"You see, we've got asthma. And the local contractors couldn't get it done before we got here. And so, we . . . well . . . we did our best to . . . well . . ." And my voice shook a little and eventually trailed off in defeat. I asked him what I should do about the roof.

"The inn's open."

"The inn?"

"Yep. But I'd cover the furniture with sheets first. Just in case."

"Sheets?" I might not have been audible at this point.

Finally he seemed to take pity on me and gave me his brother-in-law's name.

"Your brother-in-law? Oh, thanks . . . Is he the closest volunteer firefighter?" My voice surged with hope.

"Nope. But he's a pretty good roofer."

146

• • •

Sometime after we moved here we visited the local church. Pretty much all Dorset had was a church, a post office, a couple of inns, and the country store. At this stage, we had already managed to sneak dogs into the Dorset Inn for a short-term (unauthorized) residency, bought the country store, and become a source of gossip at the post office counter. Church seemed like a must see.

Now, in our city lives we had been more the Ethical Society/Unitarian types. John and I had grown up in families with significant religious commitments, sure, but in our adulthoods . . . not so much. We were more Church of the *Sunday New York Times/Face the Nation* Conference. Our notion of Sunday mornings had a lot more *Meet the Press* than Meet the Congregation, but we had come to this new place to live with intention. So, maybe our intention could include a community with their eyes on that guy with his eyes on the sparrow.

Our new town was home to a beautiful United Church of Christ. It sat just past the Dorset Green; a white marble bell tower looking every inch New England. We had known a few folks around St. Louis who were UCC, and it had always seemed very liberal. Besides, it was a five-minute walk from our front door.

We went to a church coffee hour and did the

expected socializing. It was nice enough, but not entirely our cup of tea. Hannah, the social one in our group, had done some exploring, though. She had been looking in the pews and discovered that there were cards there asking if we would like a visit. As a matter of fact, a visit sounded lovely to our churchgoing neophyte. In fact, since we were new in town, it would be great if we could meet lots of people. So she filled out a visitor card.

In each pew.

In each row.

Apparently, she imagined the whole town stopping by to say hello. Maybe they'd each bring a dish. It would be fun.

The church deacons must have imagined that someone in our house was spiritually at death's door. Or possibly being held. Against their will. In the attic.

So after our foray into the arms of the Church, there very quickly came a call from the church secretary who was setting up a pastoral visit from the right reverend. Okay, I'm always up for meeting new folks. We told her that we'd be glad to visit with the reverend on Tuesday evening.

The reverend stopped by and we led him into the living room. We served warm drinks and cookies. It was festive. At least it started out that way.

The rev decided to jump into the conversation by asking us to "talk about your spiritual lives."

Well.

Okay.

Probably shouldn't bring up Tim Russert and Bob Schieffer for this part. Still, it was a reasonable question coming from a minister. So I felt compelled to explain.

"We're not exactly deacon material, Reverend."

He wanted explanations. I've always been the main talker here, so I kept going.

"I became a Unitarian because . . . well, the Jesus stories didn't work for me anymore. I grew up with an intense Methodist mother. We were in the church every time the doors opened. It was our lives. But when I got older . . . Well, the patriarchal structure of the Church was a problem for me. I'm not much of a seen-but-not-heard type of person." He seemed to be with me, so I kept on.

"You know, for me Jesus seems like a very cool guy in the Gandhi model . . . a child of God in much the same way that I am. Or you are. Sort of an old pagan view."

John sat there with his mouth hanging open. Apparently, he had planned to offer the minister another cookie . . . perhaps a top-off on his drink . . . not a theological view that put the Savior on par with a fun guy that you'd invite to parties because he mingled well. But I (smugly, to be honest) felt that I was living my new life now, and it was a life with honesty and truth in it.

Then the reverend chimed in, and I will never forget this as long as I live, I swear I'm not making it up, that he "wasn't much of a Jesus guy himself."

Uh-huh.

Now John and I both stared agape. He went on. "You know, I think of Jesus as a musician with perfect pitch." Now that, I loved. What a perfectly delightful man. We had landed in the most perfect place in the world. What a great home for us. What a community.

Only then, he came back. Twice.

Once, he took our older son to lunch. Benjamin was struggling with the college adjustment, and this gentle minister invited him to lunch to talk about it. I just could not believe how lucky we were.

But then there was the third visit. We had all gotten sick in the way that families do. First, one of you has the sniffles and then all five of you are miserable in a loud, messy, haven't-bathed-in-a-week sort of way. And this is a small town. A very small town. So of course it got around to the minister that we were all under the weather. And a minister's whole darned raison d'etre pretty much requires that he visit the sick, right? When I was a kid in the Methodist church, a parishioner couldn't so much as cough twice without my mother and I on Casserole Patrol, knocking at their door. This is the way of churches everywhere. And it's a good thing. Really, it is. Mostly.

So our newly found spiritual shepherd very

sweetly brought us pea soup. Of course, he didn't call. It's a small town. Why bother with a phone call when you could just step up the lane—a five-minute walk—and bring food? So he walked. Into our yard. There, of course, he met our dogs.

Stuart, the elderly Cairn Terrier, was still not settled into this foreign space. This was a place where strange men with hammers and drills wandered about fixing something or other all the time. These hammerers and drillers had bothered Stuart, but generally one of us was there to soothe him. Not today. Today we were all inside as he patrolled the yard. And this . . . this man with his soup . . . was prancing right up to the house through the patrol route. This was just too much. This was the line in the sand. Stuart's Scottish temper would take no more.

And so, Stuart barked. He barked as ferociously as he knew how in a clear, indisputable warning that this was trespassing. Up with this he would not put. But apparently the reverend put his trust in faith, which as it turns out was a mistake. Stepping around Stuart, the minister walked right up to the door. The *door.* So Stuart did the only thing that any self-respecting terrier could do. He bit the right reverend.

Okay, so he bit him repeatedly.

On the ankle. Possibly the heel.

And the sweet, "not much of a Jesus guy" minister with medicinal pea soup in hand kicked

Stuart.[2] He kicked our dog. In our dog's own *yard*. Okay, so he was provoked. But still. It was, after all, Stuart's yard. It was next to his very own house. And this guy just . . . cavalierly, even, just kicked the little guy.[3]

Well of course he did. I mean, the guy is a United Church of *Christ* preacher, for Christ's sake, and he goes around pandering to the pagans by saying he's "not much of a Jesus guy." What did he expect? We had moved to a place that we knew practically nothing about, except that it was pretty. We worried about what else we didn't know. I mean, we moved to what I now saw was clearly a Republican town in an otherwise deeply blue state, and now we had a dog-kicking preacher who would apparently say anything to get new members.

Not much of a Jesus guy? I figured Jesus was probably glad.[4] Such blasphemy! The whole episode was a mark of how out of my mind I was becoming that I could even think such a thing about this sweet man who had brought us soup and tended our boy.

---

2. That soup was really good, though. To give credit where it is due.

3. Okay, maybe it was more of a reflexive jerk.

4. To be fair, the reverend is known as a dog lover. And he was bringing us soup. And our dog did bite him. So in an equitable world the blame perhaps should have fallen on us. I was just in no mood for justice.

• • •

So I might have a little trouble with church during most of the year. Or maybe that's just Stuart—I blame his Scottish Calvinist bloodline. But during Christmas—then I believe. It's the time of year when believing . . . in something . . . feels essential. I loved going to church as a little girl with candles in hand, singing "Silent Night." And even now, not quite completely believing in the whole story, or anyway in all that has come along afterwards . . . I love it still.

And Santa, in him I certainly believe. When my kids got older and started to wonder about the story, I told them that Santa lives in each of our hearts. He's the spirit of Christmas. This might be a little bit pagan, but somehow, for me, his spirit is just as real as that little baby in the manger. The differences in their stories seem less important to me than their similarities. Each offers redemption. Each inspires us to be better to one another—to love, to imagine, to warm ourselves by the fire with our family.

Well . . . with our chosen family, anyway. Sometimes we choose the family that we were born with. Sometimes we choose the family that came after. I learned a long time ago that you get two chances at family. As little children, we don't have much choice in how it all works out around us, but as you grow older you get a second shot. The whole mother-child bond . . . the family . . . works from both sides. And so I was determined that this time, as a mother, it would be happy and whole.

And by golly, it has been. This time I got the lucky hang of happiness. And now, with these people whom I chose, we believe. At Christmastime especially. We believe, for instance, in the goodness of butter and sugar. With sticky hands, we open presents and make cups of tea and coffee.

We snuggle under blankets and listen as the Vince Guaraldi Trio makes us want to dance like Linus and Lucy in front of the tree. And it's a wonderfully pagan tree. John and I were married under a Christmas tree many years ago, and we believe in the healing, happy power of its light and color. Its sparkle and shine. We believe.

We roll dough and eat handfuls of it raw. Eventually a few cookies get baked. We play silly games, and argue over the results. And on Christmas Eve we eat in fancy restaurants and toast this little family of ours. This is the stuff of happiness, chocolate chips, fizzy drinks, marshmallow cream, and red sprinkles. Perhaps it's all this goo that binds us together in a way that just being related never could.

A sweet friend of my Hannah's said that Christmas only makes her sad. "It's just for happy families. It makes everyone else miserable."

But there is a secret truth about family. Eventually, you get to pick a family for yourself.

And thanks to these sticky, sweet, funny, loud, rambunctious people I chose, Christmas is my favorite time of the year.

It was supposed to be a blizzard. Maybe, even, it was. At any rate, they were predicting winds of up to fifty miles per hour, a biting cold just warm enough for googobs[5] of snow, sleet, and maybe just a little hail to top it all off. And, of course, we were having a party.

It was our twentieth annual Christmas party. The guest list has changed over the years, as our single friends became our married friends and then, after the kids came, we added families to the rotation as well. Now, after our moving a thousand miles away, the whole guest list had turned over. But even as the people changed, the themes were a constant.

First, food. There was always a lot of bad but good party food. No vegetable platters for us. You may feel smug making those platters with the broccoli and the carrots and the cauliflower, but they always just wind up in the chicken yard the next day. Ours was a festival of debauchery. There were tenderloin sandwiches with balsamic onions and blue cheese nestled against cheesy

---

5. That's a meteorological term I picked up from Ben Abell of the Department of Earth and Atmospheric Sciences at Saint Louis University. It was a serious storm. I don't think he'd ruled out the possibility of Yetis.

snipped-chive potato boats and crab cakes with a rich rich remoulade. There might be fruit, sure, but it would have a dip made from cream cheese and Marshmallow Fluff, so it certainly couldn't count as healthy, either. Oh, and there must be a cheese ball straight out of my mother's 1970s kitchen, next to the mounds of fudge and chocolaty cookies. Christmas reminds us of our childhoods.

My childhood was filled with cholesterol.

Then, we would decorate the house and ourselves in full Christmas regalia. The tree was gigantic. The tinsel was plentiful. The ornaments were over the top. Each year, during our Christmas Adventure, each family member picked out a new tree ornament. There are five of us. That's a lot of ornaments.

And of course there were the carols. They were sung with enthusiasm and zest. I'm not sure that you could say they were sung on-key, but they were sung loudly so I think that's pretty much the same thing. If there was enough snow, we'd hire a horse-drawn sleigh to drive us around town so we could thrill the village with our carols and charm. It was the stuff of Dickens.

Our friends and their families were always welcome at Christmas. It was a big house with room for a lot of people. There was always more food than we could possibly eat. And if they thought that poking fun at our schmaltzy

Christmas was a good idea . . . then they were just in the wrong spot.

But that year, we were beginning to wonder if anyone would come. The word "blizzard" was being bandied about pretty freely. We felt like Rudolph would be needed to guide our friends' sleighs over these mountain roads. And, boy, did the weather come.

We got about a foot and a half of snow. Then there was the sleet. And finally, the hail. It was an icy foundation. The storm made the news even back in the Midwest, but apparently we had lived in the mountains just long enough to know that if the wind doesn't take out the power, it is just another winter in Vermont.

The plow trucks were doing their thing. The plows are a veritable army of burly coffee-drinking men keeping all of us connected through an invisible map that they seem to carry in their heads. They keep pretty perfect track of which roads need them the most. It's really something.

So almost everyone made it to the party. They came late, of course. And they stayed later, but we had hot buttered rum by the fire, which made it a very festive time indeed.

Our friend Ame's dad joined us for the first time that year. Percy had recently lost his wife of sixty-three years, and his memories of Nancy would keep her alive for all of us. He is an older southern gentleman . . . a retired psychiatrist. He is easily the most elegant looking . . . bawdiest sounding . . . eighty-six-year old I have ever met.

Percy offers up "darlin' " in two long syllables, with an accent that, it must be said, makes me swoon. Only, "darlin' " often accompanies a . . . colorful description . . . as in, "oh, darlin' he was always just a cocksucker." This might be a description that you wouldn't want to have to explain to your small children. At a Christmas party. But we loved him and he seemed to love us right back.

We had considered canceling the party, but the fire and the Christmas lights are often the only bright spots around here after about 3:30 p.m. during December. You need a tight marriage and good friends close by on those long, dark winter days. Percy had only recently moved to Vermont, but he already knew the secret to being happy here.

"Darlin'," he drawled, "go when you are invited. Bring good boots, drive slow, take blankets, carry your own salt, but by all means . . . go where the light is."

That's not bad advice, wherever you live. Darlin'.

After Christmas, winter can be hard up here. Sure, there are beautiful compensations, but a long winter is a long winter. Eventually there *is* spring, and with spring you get Easter.

When I was little, Easter was a bit of a big deal. It had all the buildup of Christmas, without all the marketing. I mean, first there was Lent. I grew up near St. Louis, and St. Louis believes in throwing quite a party as it heads into Lent. Mardi Gras isn't quite on the New Orleans scale, but it's a good time for all concerned. So, first there would be parties to kick off the season. Then you got to wave palm fronds around at church. Palm fronds. Some of my friends were Catholic, and they had to give up things like chocolate or Saturday-morning cartoons, which seemed sort of exotic to a very Protestant little Methodist girl.

During Lent, we got to wear a special robe and light candles every week as we led up to the big day. Every Sunday was a reminder that it was coming. Pretty soon it was Maundy Thursday, which was sort of morose, but filled with drama.[6] Easter was the greatest murder mystery ever told. I always imagined stormy weather (with big bass-drum thunderclaps) surrounding the disciples as they ate. We would enter the darkened church and take the nighttime Communion. It was a savage story, eating the body and drinking the blood of our Lord. There was a hint of cannibalism. It felt scarier than the monsters of Halloween ever did. This was the Real Thing.

---

6. I may have mentioned that I've always been drawn to the dramatic.

Good Friday was too depressing for words, if you hadn't skipped to the end and known how it would all turn out. We would read the story, and I would stare up at the beautiful wooden cross on the altar. My imagination would run wild.[7]

I remember, as a very little girl, looking at my book with the paintings of Jesus and the disciples. Since I was born in 1962, Jesus, with all the robes and sandals and long hair, had sort of a . . . okay . . . so, a sexy hippie look to him. To tell the truth, I guess I had a pretty big crush on him.

Then, on the big morning, my mom and I would get up very early to put on our matching home-made mother-daughter Easter dresses. My mom had been sewing for weeks. There were patent leather purses, shoes, and hats in sweet pastels. We would be at church by 6:00 a.m. for the sunrise service, singing, "Alleluia, Christ the Lord is risen again, Aaaaah-ley-luuuu-yuh!" We made a joyful noise unto the Lord, and then we drove into St. Louis for a big Easter breakfast at a fancy hotel right on the river. We hurried, too, which was kind of exciting in itself, since we weren't exactly strollers normally. But there was no time for lingering, since we had to be back for "regular church" by ten. After that, we would usually have our Easter egg hunt.

When I was nine, Mom switched things up a

---

7. Dramatic.

bit. She insisted that we have the egg hunt *before* sunrise service. This sounded like a terrible idea. But I was nine. So, blearily I ran around the yard looking for colorful eggs. I snatched them up, put them in my basket, and dashed back inside. This year, though, the eggs were plastic. That was unusual. I opened them up and found that inside each egg was a pair of earrings. Six weeks before, my mother had let me get my ears pierced. At the six-week mark, I could switch to real earrings, and Mom had picked out several pairs for me. I got ladybugs, little gold hoops, and, best of all, tiny gold crosses. They were no bigger than my pinky fingernail, but were especially for church that day. I was thrilled. It felt a little like I was engaged to Jesus.

Nowadays, my family and I have the big breakfast and the (let's be honest) pagan egg hunt, without all the alleluias. When we moved to Vermont, I was reading Thomas Merton and looking, searching, really, for the differences between spirituality and religion. I missed the community of the church family I had grown up with. Yet Christianity wasn't working for me, as it had in various ways throughout my early life. The sunrise service and Easter earrings weren't quite enough anymore. My belief in what I can only call God has deepened and expanded as my life has grown closer to the natural world in this old, beautiful place. Still, I fail to connect that with "religion."

My children, lacking a foundation of religious teaching, grew up, instead, with a series of questions and conversations. They had long sessions picking apart difficult problems, rather than comforting, if sometimes grizzly, stories of sacrifice and resurrection. For them, science provides all the answers they seem to need. My own once strong and guiding faith no longer fits. When I think of the way the Gospels are strung together with all of those other biblical tales, in a seemingly haphazard and often ridiculous way, I have to wonder how such a flawed text could have been inspired handiwork. How could it produce anything like a glorious outcome?

In this family, we live our lives with intention. We try to figure out what the right things are to do, and then we try to do them. Even without the reassuring framework of a church, we try to see the right road. We try to find the strength to take it. I am proud of our integrity and of the way we live: mostly, in love and grace.

But all the same, especially in spring, I miss the alleluias. I'm glad for the resurrection story and the rebirth of nature. I feel compelled to sing about it, and to do a little dance to encourage the crocuses. Often, though, I get caught up in my mud season, that time when it still gets dark early and the days are filled with questions. Like

Thomas from those old Bible stories, I am cold, and I doubt.

Of course, I can predict the future. I have a calendar. Warmer days will come. After all, these aren't the first doubts, nor are they relentless questions. They have come before. So have some answers.

One Sunday, late in one of the first long winters after we'd moved here, my shoes got stuck in the mud. Pulling them up, I caught sight of tiny little shoots of what would, deep into summer, become tiger lilies. They had been right under there, hidden away in the dark all along . . . waiting. Just waiting.

Alleluia.

⫸ Chapter Eight ⫷

The HQCS

For a long time, we thought the Lovely Quaint Country Store would be our happy ending. I mean, it was right here in this perfect little village, with our lovely home, and these gorgeous mountains. Being at the center of town life would be grand. We could stitch ourselves into the fabric of this historic place, and maybe make a little profit while we were at it. The store had so much potential. The right family could really make it sing and dance. We had that notion that maybe we could even franchise these stores out to other places all over the country, bringing a bit of Vermont happiness to folks who'd never experienced this little slice of heaven. At least that was the idea right up until the night I sent Davy Crockett into the dwarf cellar to fight a monster that turned downtown Dorset into an ice rink.

Peltier's opened bright and early at seven every morning. Bill and Bruce, two of our favorite regulars, were there way before that.

Opening the store meant greeting the day, like it or not, near dawn. The opener would arrive at around 5:30 a.m. for the ritual brewing of the coffees, opening of the side door, and the carrying in of the bundles of papers left by delivery guys in the predawn hours. We brewed four different coffees each morning. The coffee aroma was welcome and a little overwhelming. There was a Green Mountain blend, a caffeine-free variety, hazelnut, and then something exotic for the rotating fourth spot. The pots sat on an old faded-green Hoosier cabinet. We would fill the cream pitchers and pour the first cup of coffee before heading into the wine room, where we sorted the daily paper deliveries.

Papers at the store took a bit of organizing. There were three local papers, which is probably a little unusual nowadays. Additionally, Dorset is a village filled with part-time residents enjoying their second homes. This translated into a demand for the hometown papers of some of our residents. There were deliveries from New York, Boston, and other points well beyond the Green Mountains.

With the aroma of coffee and newsprint heavy in the air, we would head to the kitchen to start the baked goods. In the mornings, there was always someone firing up the oven and mixing batter. We had muffins[1] in the oven alongside croissants[2] and all those baked goodies folks needed in order to face the day.

---

1. Corn, bran, blueberry, and cranberry.
2. Chocolate and spinach feta, in addition to the buttery standard variety.

At about six, either Bill or Bruce would slip in the side door, flip on the lights, and fill his first cup of the day. Within a few minutes, the other one would show up and the "real" day could begin.

"So, you decided to sleep in this morning. You feeling okay?"

The question was, of course, the prerogative of the early arrival. And whether it was Bill or Bruce, we heard it every morning. Now, they had raced to get there, but the person who arrived first inevitably implied that he had been up for hours. Maybe he had been milking the cows . . . feeding the pigs . . . saving the world . . . and now he was casually stopping in for a cup of joe at Peltier's on his way home. Now, nevermind that these conversations happened every single morning, in driving rain with slickers and hoods, or right in the middle of a windy snow-blowing nor'easter in gloves, boots, and hats. The theme was always that "I've been up since the roosters. Oh, and I already read the paper besides."

We weren't really innocent in the competition. We would casually drape a paper on the counter so that the first arrival had a chance to scan the headlines before getting ready to pounce on his friend.

"Did you see what that president of ours did yesterday? I am telling you, we need to impeach him and try him for war crimes."

"Really? This president you're talking about is the best we've ever had. People have jobs and the market is roaring along. You can't have any complaints about that."

"Oh, it's not the market that worries me. It's all those boys and girls in khaki! The man is a war criminal, I'm telling you."

Just another[3] morning in Dorset.

Vermont is a strange place. Being a "real" Vermonter is important. Of course, no one who actually *lived* in the village was originally from the village. I guess there had probably been some babies born here since our arrival, which meant that they could say they were from Dorset. But locals . . . *real* locals . . . are rare. Most folks in Dorset come from somewhere else. After 9/11, the housing prices soared here. People were looking for quiet and rural, I suppose. And then, the second-home trade has always made it tough for native Vermonters to stay in this town. If folks from New York, Boston, and Chicago[4] are willing to buy houses at outrageous prices, it makes it nearly impossible for locals to afford homes here. Bill and Bruce were transplants, like the rest of us.

Bill and Mona, his wife, had vacationed in Dorset for many years. A near-fatal motorcycle

---

3. Every.
4. And, I suppose, obviously, St. Louis.

accident convinced them that a calmer, slower life was the sensible course. They were warm, lefty liberals, involved in activities all over town. They loved the summer theater, and they could be counted on at the firemen's carnival as well. Bill had rakish, wavy hair and a cool jacket.[5]

Bruce was briefly (which seems appropriate) a Comet. He had been an actual drummer with Bill Haley and the Comets. As exciting as that was, his family thought that it was probably a dead-end career, so he decided to join the army instead. Because that Haley fella . . . he's just a flash in the pan, right? Oh well.

Now, Bruce was a kindly, right-leaning conservative, who had retired from his Connecticut landscaping business. He'd come to Vermont wooed by customers who had sung the praises of Vermont's beauty and slow pace. He raised llamas now, and bought tractors for the seemingly unending mowing going on over at his smallholding. He had close-cropped white hair and a wardrobe that was perfect . . . in Connecticut.

What these two had in common was a love of the early morning, coffee, and a cheerful argument. Bruce had probably never been all that political until he had met Bill. Bill provided a safe venue and a friendly adversary. And they seemed to like us. We didn't interrupt their routine, and

---

5. All of them. If there was a cool jacket, Bill had it.

at least the coffee and the muffins were unchanging. Of course, I now understand that, from their vantage at the coffeepots, the rest of the place was obviously (and quickly) going straight to hell.

One of the things about running the store (into the ground) was that we began to lose staff. Bruce, up with the roosters anyway, commandeered a stool, folded papers, and greeted every customer who walked through the door. He was unfailingly friendly, and we were . . . well . . . sort of losing our . . . extroversion? Minds?

Sales were falling faster than we could count them. One of our first "improvements" had been to install an extravagantly expensive computer system. There were gobs of lovely reports. It could calculate our cost of goods sold if we changed a pricing by a penny or a percentage. It could project profits and recommend loss leaders. It really was a thing of beauty.

What it couldn't do was disguise the facts. The program was tied directly into our point-of-sale system, so it always told us exactly, to the penny, even to the minute . . . the unvarnished truth. Unfortunately, the truth in all those fancy reports was that the monthly sales . . . the daily sales . . . hell, all of the fucking sales, were down from last year. The truth sometimes uses strong language.

First, during the Great Bread Boycott, we were

down just a god-awful 20 to 30 percent. That 30 percent seemed like gangbusters when you compared it with the following year, when Vermont had the rainiest summer in the history of recorded rainfall. It would have been impossible to believe that we were at a negative (yes, negative) 70 percent,[6] if we hadn't been the only people actually in the store when we ran that report. Of course, when you combined all that with the store's price tag,[7] due diligence that had more in common with fortune-telling than accounting, a little bad luck, and our total and completely lamebrain mismanagement, we had really . . . to use the technical term . . . shit the bed.

I applied my vast business experience and acumen to the situation, and I knew at least one thing that I had to do.

I stopped running the reports.

They gave me a headache.

During all this, Bill and Bruce were our reprieve. They were unfailingly nice to the few people who still came into the store . . . I think they even came into the store to buy things, though the reports I'd stopped running might not show that. Bill began to handle the back of the store, working the coffee counter and the aisles.

---

6. Feel free to use the term "catastrophic" here.
7. Which had very little to do with financial worth.

Bruce worked the front. They were the picture of friendly, happy customers. I think they planned to start a trend.

Now, with so few customers in the store as we were losing money hand over fist, you'd probably think that we valued every person who walked over our threshold. They would be precious to us. We would be tripping over ourselves to be gracious to them. Only, unaccountably, really, we weren't.

The people who weren't coming into the store were the ones we were mad at. This Horrible Quaint Country Store, or HQCS, was going to destroy us financially . . . possibly psychologically . . . and it was all . . . okay, not really . . . but it seemed like it was all their fault. But, of course, those folks weren't coming in for us to be angry with, so we were grumpy with the poor people who actually did try to buy things from us.

You might imagine that this would make even fewer people come into the store than before, which would be disastrous for the business. And, you know what? You would be right about that. It did. But apparently all that taught us was that the remaining customers must have something dread-fully wrong with them. I mean, who would actually shop with *us?* These people must be terrible. So we began to loathe them, too.

Of course, the remaining customers were becoming a little pissy, now that you mention it.

And, true, they did have a point. Sometimes our shelves might have been a little sparse. Perhaps our products were maybe a little below the level of excellence that they expected and that we had been aiming for. And possibly . . . just maybe . . . there was a chance that the help was a little . . . well . . . surly.

Strangely, they noticed these things.

Okay, but can I just say that it sure seemed like they noticed these . . . little challenges . . . *before* they had actually happened? Really.

As an example, before things had gotten bad . . . okay, before they had gotten catastrophically bad, we had ordered in these organic peaches. From New Jersey. It *is* the Garden State. Anyway, we had these peaches shipped in just after picking—daily. Yes, it was true that they were about four bucks a pop. But look, they were organic! And we had them in these cute little baskets with red-and-white cloth napkins in the bottom. And we tied gingham ribbons on the handles. They were juicy, fresh, and ripe.

"Hmmm . . . Is this peach meeeeeealy?" sang out the Dylanesque voice of one of the few customers shopping our HQCS.

The sales hadn't quite dropped out from under us yet. I mean, they weren't stellar, but we were still in the almost-optimistic early days. Perhaps we thought that we could afford to lose the kinds of customers who weren't happy with us. We'd moved to Vermont for the beauty and the love, after all. So when the peach critic cried out, I might have answered, "Why, yes. Yes it is! Mealy. Boy, hehehe, we sure can't fool *you*." My voice might have edged slightly out of friendly and into mildly manic.

"Why, this peach . . . This peach here . . . it's just mealy as shit. Luckily, it is also really expensive! Want a dozen?"

Surprisingly, no, she didn't think she did now that I mentioned it. And, perhaps less surprisingly, we never saw her again. But that was okay, because at about that time we started to get the money throwers.

The money throwers were a group of Republican guys (they were all men) in pink pants. Okay, they were golfers, so I guess the pink pants were somehow appropriate. Not that I have a problem with guys . . . believe me, I love guys . . . or with golfers, either, come to think of it . . . or with Vermont Republicans, which seem to be of the happy old Rockefeller variety. Some of my best friends are Vermont Republican guys . . . well, it's true, actually, they are . . . though I'm not sure if they own pink pants. Anyway, all that aside, these guys would wander up to the register with a *Bennington Banner* or a *Wall Street Journal*, and when they got to the register they would cavalierly throw their money down. Now, I don't want you to confuse this with a toss. This was a slap . . . literally and figuratively, actually. THWACK! Down goes the cash. And then they would stand there staring, seemingly in exasperation, while they waited for us to pick up the cash and give them their change.

And how did we respond? Did we throw their change down, too, you might wonder? Really? You're still wondering? Haven't you been keeping up?

Then things started to really go south.

"There really isn't very much tuna on my tuna sandwich."

"Well, ma'am, I sure am sorry about that, but as you might have noticed we are going bankrupt here. That's why we have no help"—as I gestured around the store—"and the shelves are kind of bare. But, don't you worry, we think we have solved the problem!" My voice might have taken on a high-pitched, chirpy, clearly fake soprano as I answered that "We are putting out less food and charging more! See, we hired this fancy business consultant, and that was his advice. I think it's a winner! Don't you?"

We may have been just a bit crabby.

In fact, it is just barely conceivable that I actually told one woman, using my outside voice and everything, that I thought, perhaps, she might be happier shopping elsewhere. I might have literally taken the groceries from her bag one by one and put them in the "To Be Restocked" bin. It's rumored that I might have then just quietly stared at her as she stood perfectly still, openmouthed, and slowly[8] turned to walk out of my store. In that brief moment, I was glad.

Who *were* these horrible, entitled people? Couldn't they see the cute handmade toys that we'd stocked? Had they *bothered* to walk into the restored wine room with the thoughtful collection arranged *painstakingly* by grape?! Couldn't they see the love we'd put into those *goddamned* flower boxes?! What about the *fifteen* varieties of balsamic on the shelves, huh? How about those? Hadn't they heard about our TAKE HOME SUPPERS!!!!???

Pretty soon, Bruce was asking, quietly, in a very soft, gently measured voice . . . the voice you might use with a mental patient who has escaped from the psychiatric facility only to knock on your front door . . . if he could help out with the register. Maybe we wanted to go stock the beer in the cooler?

I think he was hoping that we'd have one . . . or six . . . while we were over there.

Bruce, oddly and amazingly, found it quite easy to be nice to everyone. I mean, of course, he hadn't mortgaged his life for a Horrible Quaint Country Hole, but still. He was so nice.

---

8. And, it must be said, satisfyingly . . . haven't you ever wanted to do that?

Unfailingly cheerful. Everyone (everyone left, anyway) got a big toothy smile and a folksy joke. Well, almost everyone.

It was a rainy Tuesday and the newspapers were soaked. The delivery guy hadn't covered the bundles that morning because it was supposed to be sunny. At 3:00 a.m., he had no reason to suspect foul weather. Only, then, of course, it rained all morning, because foreshadowing can be a bitch.

By midmorning the sun had come back. We'd been yelled at by every single *Boston Globe* reader[9] in the area for the last four hours, so we figured it was time for a bit of a break. We had old friends visiting us from St. Louis, and it seemed like a little sightseeing was in order. I mean, we had employees we couldn't afford, anyway, and Bruce, who was carefully keeping us away from personal interactions and sharp objects, so we headed to the waterfall.

Despite everything that was going wrong at the store, surprisingly . . . maybe even amazingly . . . we were still pretty infatuated with Vermont. It was probably the only thing that kept us sane . . . or sane-ish.

One day Benjamin had come home and told us that he'd found a waterfall. It was a kid thing. All the teenagers knew about it.

---

9. Point of interest, *Globe* readers are a lot less forgiving than their *New York Times* counterparts. Who knew?

"We should hike up there together. It'll be fun," he contended.

Since moving to Vermont, I'd had my share of mountain hikes. When a person mentions a hike, I had learned that this was not to be mistaken for an invitation to walk. Hikes and walks have nothing in common.

A city walk might be brisk. It might meander through a park. It seldom caused me to reach for my inhaler, or required a long soak in a really hot tub. I'd discovered that, in Vermont, a walk required new shoes. City shoes wouldn't cut it. The new shoes I'd bought gave me blisters. A waterfall did sound nice, but he had used two dreaded words that I didn't trust: "hike" and "up." These aren't particularly pretty words by themselves, but if you put them together . . . in Vermont . . . they are the harbingers of doom.

Despite all the store-related craziness, summer in Vermont is quite a marvelous thing. The days are warm and sunny, but the mornings are usually cool enough for a cape. I had lots of capes of various weights from all the years that I'd spent dreaming of living up here. Every autumn trip was cause for a new one, and wearing a cape in the summer was thrilling beyond my wildest imagination.[10]

10. To be fair, I also hadn't imagined that I would be wearing them in layers over my flannel nightgown during winter mornings. When we were cutting back on expenses like heating oil, I watched my breath floating away in the kitchen. That might have been a bit less idyllic.

Benjamin finally persuaded me to try the waterfall. It was an easy little hike, he promised. I'd been tricked before, but I was game. As it turns out, it was actually a gentle hike beside rushing water. We drove to Pawlet, the next town over, and parked on the side of the road beside the sign for the Harmon Mint. Vermont made its Revolutionary currency at the Mint when we were our own little country. Outsiders, and some insiders, too, for that matter, still call this place the Republic of Vermont for its fierce independence and often wildly liberal politics. The Mint is about all that's left of our independent republic. And, more importantly, the sign for the Mint is where you park for the waterfall.

We piled out of the car and walked along the guardrail. When we got to the place where the weeds were trampled down, I hiked up my skirt and climbed over. I'd been wearing these gypsy skirts for most of my life, and saw no reason for a few mountains to change a lifetime of fashion choices. The men up here seemed amused and flirted cheerfully[11] despite my ample backside, so I figured that it wasn't all that different here after all. But these walks . . . or hikes . . . left holes in my skirts, and in my confidence. In the effort to get my mind off the store, I was willing to sacrifice a skirt to a guardrail.

---

11. Like men everywhere.

We ambled down a little incline, smack into a vast cornfield. Benjamin led the way, and we found a walking path between rows. It was getting deeper into summer and the corn was high. The view was corn. Lots of corn. I wouldn't have been surprised to see Shoeless Joe Jackson. Then, as quickly as it appeared, the field receded. We crept onto a woodsy trail alongside loud water. The woods were thick, so we couldn't see the river. But there was no mistaking the sound. We walked through piney woods with moss underfoot, and smelled the blanket of soft pine needles. It might have been an enchanted forest. And then, right there in front of us, we happened on Benjamin's waterfall.

Ten minutes from the highway we found a beautiful three-story waterfall. It was rushing fast from the heavy spring melt. I caught my breath and sat on a fallen tree. The dappled light washed and waved through the tops of the tree branches. It was the most beautiful place I had ever been. And it was here, right where I lived. It was a five-minute drive and a ten-minute walk (I mentally revised this gentle climb to a walk . . . not a hike). John and I could drag thermoses of coffee up here and neck like teenagers. Teenagers aren't the only ones who get to neck in public, after all. And we could spend hours up here with Eli while he chased frogs and lizards. Hannah could bring her stacks of magazines, or maybe those vampire books. I imagined Benjamin making a beautiful watercolor. We could picnic here on lazy summer days.

And we did. We still do, actually. It all came true.

When the bills were keeping us up at night, and the banker was calling us every morning to decide whether we could continue our overdraft just a little more for a little longer, I would come up here. Sometimes I would hang my head over the side until all my senses were filled with the woods and the water. I could block out everything up here and, if only for a while, remember that this had all been a deliberate choice. We'd intended to find a new life. We'd . . . okay, maybe I'd . . . been a little bored in our old life.[12] We certainly weren't bored anymore.

It turns out that we'd been right about building a deeper connection to the natural world. There was nothing much that hot, thick coffee drunk from a thermos next to a waterfall on a sunny summer day couldn't fix. Life was old here. There was a sense of perspective, living next to trees that had seen the American Revolution. This village had houses older than our country. Despite the messes we were making over on Church Street—and boy, were they messes—we were also finding a new way to live.

---

12. Note to self: Beware of boredom.

After a particularly mean customer, or a crummy test, or maybe even a teenage broken heart, we'd all come to the waterfall. We'd bring our dearest friends and relatives on visits. The waterfall was ours. It became a symbol. We didn't have to run out and buy something new when we felt cheated or when we felt lost. We didn't need a stiff drink, either. We had everything we needed in each other. This simple, beautiful place where we lived would feed us. It would nurture our souls.

We didn't have many cinemas or music houses. There were no malls, and no wine-soaked gallery openings. But there were waterfalls and mountains. It would fill us up. Well, it would if we could just figure out what to do about that damned store.

So we'd taken our friends here, to this perfect place. We spent a couple of hours counting blessings and recharging. And then, feeling refreshed and hopeful again, we headed back to the store.

That, as it turns out, was probably an error.

But we did, we headed back. That break had been just what we needed. Sharing a beautiful place with good friends on a nice day. Just what the doctor ordered. And as we approached the store I could see that there were even a couple of cars in our parking spaces. Customers. Huh. That's not something we saw every day. There was even a lady getting gas at our pumps. She was all dressed up, too. It looked like she might have an appointment. I remember thinking, "Doesn't she look nice." And maybe . . . just maybe . . . we'd be able to pay our gas bill that week.

We walked in and greeted Bruce from his perch behind the counter. I decided that I was feeling well and whole enough to take a turn at the register. Bruce wandered over to the front door, sipping his coffee and enjoying a peaceful moment. Well, a moment anyway. Suddenly Bruce started making horrible sounds. I had no idea what was happening, but it turns out that it was a scream. This scream started way back in the throat. I thought he must be having a heart attack. But he wasn't grabbing his chest. Bruce was staring out the front door, horrified.

I ran around the counter to see what was going on. John came from the back of the store. Customers, the few whose cars were parked outside, ran over as well. The ladies working in our kitchen crowded in, too, wearing their aprons and startled expressions. You remember that nice-looking lady who had been getting gas out front a minute ago? She'd finished pumping her gas and had driven away. That seems normal enough, I know. But she was in the middle of Church Street and seemed to be dragging something along behind her car. And there was a kind of white fluff . . . everywhere. For just a second, I thought it was snowing. I mean, I'd be amazed too with a little quick summer snow. Does it snow in the summer in Vermont? No? Hmmm.

Only, I was a little confused about what our gas pump was doing. In the middle of the street. Slowly, my brain began to piece together the scene. The sprinklers over our gas pump . . . well, our former gas pump . . . were going off. They were spewing water and fire-retardant foam in every direction. That nice lady who'd bought gas . . . she'd bought the gas, all right. And in a hurry, apparently, she'd forgotten to disconnect the hose from her car. So now she was driving away.

With the hose still attached.

Dragging our gas pump right down the middle of town.

And gasoline was flooding Church Street.

From our parking lot.

Oh. My. God.

I looked around and saw that a handful of local workers, who'd run in for a soda pop on their afternoon break, were all standing around outside taking in the scene, chatting, and . . . *smoking!*

Calm, in control, always friendly, Bruce screamed and ran outside, waving his arms maniacally.

"Oh no! Stop! Stop!! Stop!!!!!"

The driver stopped. The smokers stopped, gingerly stubbing out their cigarettes in a guarded way. Everybody, really, sort of stopped. In fact, everything stopped. It was a bizarre still-life with gasoline.

The driver slowly got out of her car, looking anguished as the gasoline began sloshing around her feet. Neighbors up and down the street, alerted by all the screaming, presumably, came out on their porches. No one said a word. Except for John. John, my quiet, steady husband, said practically the only bad words I have ever heard him utter.

Quietly. Without inflection, but clearly audible to all of us gathered round, John said, "We. Are. Completely. Fucked."

We were.

We called 911. Finally this would be the right time. And this time, they came. They helped us clean up the spill, but they really didn't know the first thing about gasoline spills. They are a volunteer fire department, so not everyone is trained on all the possibilities. Rogue bats and wandering bears they've got covered. Real environmental hazards are a little lower on the training regimen. But they were there and they helped. We all did our best.

Then we realized that we should call the state environmental people. That's right. And they were glad that we had called.

"Was anyone hurt? Everyone okay?"

"We're all fine," I assured them.

"Great. We'll see you in a few days."

Right. Tiny state. Hardly any people. A "few days" it is. Meanwhile, no gas pumps would mean no gas sales. Gas was, of course, one of the main reasons that people still shopped at the store. They'd fill up, and while they were here they'd take a look in the store. Great.

Before long, the "environmental disaster" became just one more story that we told. It would usually end with "At least there was insurance" or possibly "Thank God nobody got hurt." Occasionally we'd even throw in "Could have been worse." We packed on the bromides, but at least it was summertime. There were a few tourists, still, and we lived in one of the most beautiful places on earth. These were the meditations I clung to.

We were heading into the kind of weekend when there was only one thing left to do, so we did it. Our friends Ellen and Roger Questel live on the Battenkill River in Sandgate, Vermont. We had long talked about floating the river together someday. That day had come. We needed a little beauty and a whole bunch of laughs about then. We got gobs of both.

We went to the inner tube place and rented enough tubes for the four adults, our kids, and our kids' friends. We had Aline, Hannah, Eli, and Eli's best friend, Timmy, along for the trip.

Someone might have mentioned that the river was freezing. In fact, our friend Ellen, who is tiny, by the way, showed up in a wet suit. A wet suit? I giggled about that. Until I got in. Then I looked at her with a new respect. A respect that verged on awe. Teeth-chattering awe, but awe.

Floating down the river was such fun. We laughed, and paddled. And of course, it was beautiful on the water. The river was a little low in spots as it sometimes gets, but that wasn't much of a problem until several hours in when, with tired and cold muscles, we hit a run of shallow rapids.

The rapids were hard to traverse, partly because of the shallow places, but also because the currents were so fast that standing and walking or swimming through them wasn't easy. Everyone struggled in a good-natured, happy kind of way. Until one of us—okay, me—actually got, well . . . a little stuck.

I mean, there was fast-running water, but it wasn't very deep. And then there were all those pointy rocks and . . . well, my ample backside. I just could not move. This, as you've probably guessed, was a source of much hilarity among my floating buddies. Buddies who were at this point all through. They paused in the river, looking back at me, giggling, and waiting for me to inevitably solve the problem. And I would have, too, only every time I got unstuck, I would tumble right into another bunch of rapids, which sent me twirling and spinning and then BAM, my butt would catch on another one of those damnably sharp rocks.

Okay, it was funny. I laughed, too . . . at first. Then it got frustrating, and my butt started to hurt. My leg seemed to have developed a bright red gash. My friends up ahead were still looking pretty goldarned entertained. What exactly was their problem? Couldn't they see that I was practically drowning here? About then, I noticed that I had to pee. Oh, fine. They were all so busy laughing and having fun and I was stuck in those rocks and my store was going broke and so were we and soon we would probably have to live in a yurt alongside this very picturesque river. I decided that I would just sit there and pee, damnit. I figured at least I would be warm. I may, also, have cried. Just a little.

But, you know, something about peeing was just the magic I needed. Maybe it was the surrender, but before I knew it I was tumbling along, floating fast down the river. Peeing, sure, but gloriously unstuck. Roger reached out to slow me down, and they were all asking if I was okay. They were telling me that they had been devising a way to come back and rescue me. I loved them all again then. These were my friends. Who cared if we were going broke? It was only money. John and I had each other and our kids and Timmy and a few good friends who loved us. And they'd even rescue us while we peed in the river. It would all be okay one way or the other.

Probably.

And meanwhile I had a whole bunch of new butt jokes to tell.

Back at the store, tourists had started to wander by with a fair degree of regularity, which might be all we really needed. Sure we'd run into some bumps, but of course we had. We'd moved a thousand miles from everything we'd known and we'd started a business, besides. Naturally there would be adjustments. I'd been in business for many years, and I understood turmoil. I knew that sometimes you just have to change direction. That's all we needed—a little course correction. Turns out the river had really cleared my head.

I knew just what to do.

What this place, this Horrible Quaint Country Store, needed was a sense of hope and possibility. The town had been worried about us, and they needed reassuring. That was all, really. It just took time. People are change resistant. We just hadn't given them enough time. We would throw a party. Maybe a Fourth of July bash? Sure. This was a great idea. We could make lobster rolls and sell them out front. Maybe we could arrange a parade. There were lots of schools that I'd bet would love to make floats. Maybe the churches and local businesses could get involved. It could be a town-wide project. I got busy on the phone. I'm good on the phone.

I found a fife-and-drum unit that was just itching to march.[13] I called the state Veterans Affairs Office and sure enough there were groups of retired soldiers from practically every war who would participate. At the time, the nation was getting bogged down in Iraq, and Vermont had a bunch of National Guard units deployed over there. So I imagined that we could all use a little patriotic parade through the village. I also imagined free Take Home Suppers for all those Guard families on the Fourth.

We started ordering supplies. Let's see, I wondered, would a hundred pounds of lobster be enough? What, three . . . four ounces per sandwich? Let's say four. That's four per pound. We could get four hundred sandwiches. Hmm, better make it two hundred pounds. This was going to be big, after all. Everyone would come. We would need sparklers and those growing-snake fireworks. Dorset didn't technically allow fireworks, but I'd heard lots of people talking about driving over to New Hampshire to get their supply. We would just stock the safe stuff. The town would approve. I mean, what's the harm, right?

We posted signs in the store, and got big red, white, and blue bunting. We hung it early to really get people in the mood. This was going to be a

---

13. Aren't they all?

real locals event. We were talking it up to everyone. *Peltier's First Annual Old Fashioned Fourth of July Parade!* It was just what we all needed.

Kitty, an older lady who lived across the street from the store, even got into the act. She was very active in the local church, and she offered to talk about the parade during church announcements on Sunday.

"Ellen, my grands are going to be here; so you let us know what we can do to help. This sounds like fun."

That was that. If I had Kitty Hittle's approval, I was golden. Maybe I should get three hundred pounds of lobster. Two-fifty, anyway. And then there would be the tourists. I went back to my catalogs. Pretty soon, we were unloading bags of water balloons and children's fishing poles. I'd had this idea that maybe we could have a little fishing derby down at the pond for the kids. There were barrels on the front porch now filled with those poles and kites and beach balls. My, how festive we looked.

Then my banker stopped by. He'd heard about the big July project, and I figured he must want to congratulate us. Wouldn't it be nice if he wanted to congratulate us? Turned out, that wasn't exactly what he wanted. I was waiting for Rick, the handyman working on the floors in front of the produce section. Rick was setting up orange cones, and I was standing guard. We wanted the place all shipshape for the July party, so we'd called Rick to work on some of the old wood floors. There were some soft boards here and there, and we'd decided that they needed replacing. Of course, this was to be expected in a building that was two hundred years old. Of course it was. Eventually, Rick got the cones up and strung those little flags partitioning off the work zone. I headed up front to welcome Mr. Bruce Fenn.

Bruce had grown up in Dorset. He knew everyone, and everything about this town. Bruce was getting close to retirement, and he had literally seen it all. As a banker, he was a good friend to have.

"Ellen, I have been hearing about your party."

I beamed. His office was located in Brattleboro now, which was about an hour and a half away. If news of our party had traveled to him, we might need more lobster than I thought.

He was smiling, but it wasn't a comfortable smile. I wondered if he was feeling all right. I offered him some tea.

"What I am wondering about, kiddo, is whether or not you have gotten a permit."

I was puzzled. I mean, we were just a little village. What did I need a permit for exactly?

Apparently we needed a permit for the parade thingy. Sure. But that's okay because I had already thought of that. We didn't have any "regular" police officers in town, but our electrician, Theron, was Constable.[14] I'd already called to ask him if he could block off the street. I figured we could use some of the volunteer firemen in town, too. I wouldn't even call 911 first. Theron thought that he probably could block off the street fairly easily, although some kids had snatched his orange cones as a prank. I promised to donate some new ones if he would come. I was sure he would. Theron was a real doll.

"Well, Ellen, I happened to hear from someone over at the town manager's office and she was concerned. Said they keep hearing about a parade but you haven't been to a selectmen hearing to get approval."

Oh.

That was easily fixed. I would go. What, after all, could possibly be the big deal? We had World War Two veterans lined up to march. This was going to be a wonderful and wholesome family event. Who could possibly object?

"You know, Manchester has a carnival and fireworks and so this might compete with their doings over there."

Manchester was the next town over. A little town competition could be a good thing. Our selectmen surely wouldn't care what the guys in

---

14. In Vermont, this isn't as strange a sentence as you might expect.

Manchester thought, would they? I thought Bruce was worrying over nothing much, and I told him so.

"Then there's the problem of dates. I think the selectmen maybe meet . . . second Tuesday?"

Fine. . . . Oh.

Second. Tuesday.

Which was after the Fourth.

Surely they could hold an extra meeting. I would just call them all. Who were they again? Had I mentioned the World War Two veterans?

That was about when we heard the scream. Yes, another scream. It was high-pitched and came from the back of the store. There was Rick standing above the big gaping hole in the floor. The hole made when he had removed the boards in order to spruce things up. The kitchen staff were all standing there, too. You could always count on them to show up for the screaming. I remember seeing John's face. He looked sick. Then I looked down. There was a lady. Well, really, there was just a part of a lady. It took my mind a few minutes to process the scene.

Rick, floor-fixing handyman, looked like he had maybe been dancing with this woman. Or maybe it was a cuddle. She was swooning. Everyone was talking, and it was loud. Finally, I made out Rick's voice above the others.

"The cones! Didn't you see the cones!"

Rick gently lifted her out of the hole, and she

sat leaning against the cooler. Her leg looked wrong, kind of like a Barbie doll leg after the dogs have gotten to it.

Finally I understood what had happened. She'd fallen into the hole. I guessed she'd broken her leg, too, by the looks of things. There seemed to be a bloody gash. Rick just kept saying over and over, "How could she not see those cones?" And, frankly, that was a pretty good question. Maybe she was distracted by the beets that she was still holding on to. They were very nice beets, to be fair. We'd picked up those beets at the Pillemer farm just that morning as the sun came up over the mountains in Pawlet. There was a certain romance about them at sunrise. They looked decidedly less romantic gripped in the hands of an injured (presumably former) customer. Yep: 911. We were getting to be regulars.

When all the hubbub died down, Bruce the banker was gone. Eventually even Rick left. He was still muttering, "How could she not see the cones? There were cones."

I remembered, however, what the real problem was . . . broken legs or no. So I called the town manager's office right away.

Oh boy. This was a setback. That's all. A glitch. I promised them I would take care of it. I started calling the selectmen. I could do this. Hell, everybody loves the Fourth of July, right?

I started going down the list of selectmen.

Unfortunately, number one on the list was a prominent pink-pantsed money thrower. He was . . . not sympathetic. Also, possibly not a patriot. I mean, really. It's the Fourth of July. Fine, there were more of them.

Most people did actually like us. They might think we were a little dumb. Okay. We'd surely made some silly mistakes. But we were kind of endearing too, right? "Oh those silly flatlanders," I imagined them saying. I could just call and explain. It would be fine.

The next name on the list . . . a fresh start . . . had already spoken to the pink-pantsed mafia. I heard myself explaining about the freezer full of lobster. I thought I was starting to sound a little plaintive. That wouldn't do.

I explained about the fife and drums. It was a great unit. And there would be fishing. And bunting. Did I mention the bunting? I might have been rubbing my face, though of course select-man number two couldn't really see that over the phone . . . thank God. And I thought I heard screaming again. What was with all the screaming? Where was that coming from? Oh, right. This time it was coming from me.

"There are going to be WORLD WAR TWO VETERANS!! Don't you understand?!"

I finally just had to face it. I called the veterans' group and tried to explain to the nice older lady who answered the phone that there was a tiny little complication that really couldn't possibly be considered my fault. It was hardly anything, but . . . you know . . . a technicality. And we were going to have to cancel the parade.

"Can you speak up, dear? My hearing aid needs a new battery."

"HELLO, this is Ellen Stimson." Loudly and clearly. "In Dorset. I own PELTIER'S?" If only I could include some expressive hand gestures here. But a telephone is a telephone.

"We are hosting the Peltier's First Annual Old Fashioned Fourth of July PARADE? . . ."

That, she heard.

"Oh, honey, that thing's been canceled. Those people didn't get a permit."

Every adage you could think up began to apply for us.

"Things were steadily going from bad to worse."

"When it rains, it pours."

"Damned if we did and damned if we didn't."

We were a living compendium of Murphy's Laws. Our closest friends began asking us if we had considered selling the store. Were they kidding? We had started thinking about selling the store after the first week. Quietly. Not out loud, of course.

I had gotten us into this mess and I would figure out a way to get us out. It was hard even to admit to myself how dismal our prospects were. The day the Vermont state tax guy came in and introduced himself . . . now that was a moment. We were, apparently, a little behind on our sales taxes. Oh, we filed all of the quarterly reports. We had that fancy computer system that spewed reports constantly. It even had a clock that told us what reports to run, at what time, and on what days. It was horrifically efficient. What it couldn't seem to manage, though, was putting money in the bank to support all the checks it automatically generated. Those would be the checks that loomed in piles all over my office. Truly they had been looming for a while. But I knew what to do about that.

I put them in drawers!

Then there was the day my lovely sweet banker made an appointment to visit and showed up with Tom Firliet from the "workout" section of the bank to meet us.

Work. Out.

He did workouts? Turned out they hadn't meant Pilates. So that was a bad day, too, and after those visits I was beginning to slowly admit, at least to myself, that we had a little problem.

It occurred to me that this was a serious problem now, and that I'm a problem-solving kind of person. Sure I had planned to move to New England and live a nice rural life, but it also occurred to me that we only lived four hours from New York City. New York City might just be a place that I could go to and start a business. A business to support my business. And my children. And John. And me. We were all needing some supporting just at the moment.

New York City is the home of American publishing. I had been in the book business all my life. That was something I, at least, knew how to do. There were no selectmen in pink pants floating around the publishing industry. Or not a lot of them, certainly, and most of them liked me. There had to be things that I could do that wouldn't interfere with my noncompete agreement. Selling Peltier's, while appealing, was probably not going to be straightforward. Nothing else associated with buying it or running it had been. Why would I expect selling it to be any easier? I mean, first of all, we had paid way too much. That was my fault, sure, but still. And second, since we had been busily running it straight into the ground, it was probably worth decidedly less than it had been when we had paid way too much for it a year before. And, of course, since we were new to Vermont and had no experience in this industry,[15] I had personally guaranteed all of the loans. We were upside down in the worst possible way.

Oh, and our nest egg? That carefully guarded and nurtured savings that we'd put away for our retirement? We had used that to buy the busi- ness . . . our house . . . the renovations on our

---

15. Why hadn't that rung any warning bells, I wondered.

house . . . and what food was on our table. It also had a bit to do with keeping the doors open at the HQCS, besides.

Now, we had done well in our previous lives. Honestly, if we had done nothing at all after buying the house, I could have ridden out the noncompete and lived happily without a new income for a little while. Oh, but we wanted to illustrate the importance of a solid work ethic for our children.[16] They were surely seeing that work ethic up close now. They might also get to learn about bankruptcy. Maybe even a little bit of tax law while we were at it. It was a real live Monopoly game around here. We turned over a new deed every day. We had long ago stopped passing Go! and collecting two hundred dollars. I could look at my bank balance and count the time that was left. I had never been really great at math, but even I could add. We were running out of money fast, so I had to do something fast. I headed for New York the following Monday, leaving John behind to run the store.[17]

---

16. "Work" and "ethic" are another set of words, like "hike" and "up," that should come with a warning. Warning: Extreme Caution!

17. My last act as a store owner was to order John a cute little apron in Dorset green, the color of the window shutters all over town. In fact, what the hell, I had a plan now, and I had always been lucky . . . in businesses other than HQCSes . . . so, I ordered aprons for everyone. Even Bill and Bruce. It was all going to be fine. Just you wait.

Come fall, we planned to throw the First Annual Peltier's Pumpkin Festival.[18] I figured that while I was running a new business during the week, I could run weekend events when I was home. They would be kind of fun, and they would give the store more of a presence in the village. We filled our porches with more than a hundred pumpkins. We ordered a horse and carriage with these gorgeous draft horses to take folks on wagon tours around town. And maybe I would have a real Vermonty singer/songwriter playing out on the porch next to the pumpkins. Yes, okay, it was going to cost a lot. But this place needed an investment not just of cash, but also of energy and enthusiasm. We couldn't just give up.

I knew that we had to invest so that we could make this thing work! The events were planned for Columbus Day weekend. Columbus Day always brings out lots of leaf-peeping tourists. Additionally, that was the week we were supposed to get the new gas pumps. There would be lots to celebrate. We'd have caramel-dipped apples for the kids, and we would be outside, grilling Vermonters. Vermonters, for the uninitiated, are sandwiches made from ham, Vermont cheddar, and maple syrup–dipped apple slices that are grilled on a hearty rye. Everybody working at the

18. You'll note the "First Annual" implication that these events would happen more than once. Oh, optimism.

store would be decked out in Dorset green. It would be fun. We would be ready.

On the morning of October 11th, I was really excited. The Vermont Country Store did a similar event every fall, as well. I'd always loved it. I woke at 5:00 a.m. and thought, "Here we go!" Wait? Rain? The forecast was for a bright sunshiny day. I'd checked. Seventeen times. Maybe it was just a little nighttime shower that hadn't passed all the way over yet.

I opened my computer and looked at the weather-forecast app on my desktop. The big fat smiling sun had been there for a week. October 11th = Jolly Sunny Day. Well, until this morning. Sunny Day was in retreat, replaced by Evil Foreboding Cloud with Lightning Bolts.

Whatthe? Howthe? Whenthe?

That cute little sun had been there when I went to bed, damnit. It had been fucking cheerful. And sunny.

We trudged over to the store. Friends brought tents. Gamely, because we were investing energy and enthusiasm, damnit, we set up the grill. Surely it would blow over. I kept telling everyone about the Sunny Day. It had been there all week. Promise.

Carriage Guy showed up on time. He asked for his check, and then he huddled inside beside the coffeepots. Who knows? It might clear up. Maybe the banker would show up. We could offer to take him for a ride. I told Carriage Guy about the sun icon. The Vermonty musician played inside . . . next to the misplaced bread . . . for Bill and Bruce.

I told the Vermonty musician about the sun icon too, for all the good it did. Maybe he could write a song about it? Somewhere Rick, the handyman, was still muttering about those cones, and now Ellen, the loony, couldn't stop muttering about Sunny Day on her computer.

We were all going slowly[19] insane.

Winter came, and the tourists went home. The locals were stuck with us, and we were stuck with them. I was traveling between New York and Vermont all the time now. The new business had begun to take off, and so I was dancing as quickly as I could manage between one project and another. It was exciting, sure, but also terrifying. Still, this was the path out of the forest and we just had to keep walking.

John was running the store on a day-to-day basis. Bless him. While I was off in another city, a giant, thriving city, John was sorting papers at 5:30 a.m. and keeping our HQCS running. Yes, okay, "running" may not be quite the right word. He was overseeing the collapse. And, to be honest, doing it much more sanely than I could have managed. After a certain point, the gallows humor began to set in. John would send me little

---

19. Mostly slowly.

email messages on the days that I was in New York. "Updates from the Front," we called them. He would sign them "Love, Davy."[20]

Ultimately, we tried to keep this whole experience in perspective. These were . . . rough spots . . . a few of them . . . Okay, so one after another, really. Hard times, maybe. Everyone has a rough patch, though, right? We were smart people, and we weren't afraid of hard work. We loved each other, and we were confident that we could figure it all out. Until we had the little boiler problem.

It was a weekend, and I was home. Eli, Hannah, and I had cooked up a "jammies day." We planned to start with blueberry pancakes, and really, don't a lot of great days start that way? We would build a roaring fire, and watch old movies while playing a little pinochle. Maybe we would bake some cookies. Why not? Live a little, right? John rented a big pile of movies and scheduled himself off of the Peltier's calendar so that he could snuggle in with us for a change. Things had been rough lately, and we needed a day together.

On Friday night, Julia, Peltier's most steadfast and reliable employee, had closed the store. Before she left she called to mention that the boiler seemed to be leaking a little more than

---

20. As in Crockett. Welcome to the Alamo, Ladies and Gentlemen. Has anyone seen my musket?

usual. Well, the boiler . . . the boiler was a monster. It was hidden away, deep down in the cellar. You could only get to it from a door on the outside of the store. The door was about four and a half feet high, so you had to duck your head when you visited. I suppose that two hundred years ago, Grumpy and Sleepy hadn't built for the possibility of snow . . . even in Vermont. In the early days, this had seemed charming. Charming in the way that the old wooden wagon wheel in the attic had been charming. In the store's historic beginning, hay bales were stored in what was now our attic. They would be rolled out the upper-level windows into the waiting customers' wagons. A sort of nineteenth-century drive-through. The boiler turned out to be not so charming.

The boiler hadn't come over on the *Mayflower*, but only barely. It was ancient. In addition to quarterly tune-ups from a professional, it required a series of daily ministrations to keep it going. Steps included emptying the water pan that received the hose from the Thingy, which dipped into the Jigger Doodad. It was also important to screw off the Thingamabob before you adjusted the Whatsit. Don't forget to replace the Thingamabob after you turned the Whatsit back on, or there would be hell to pay.[21] These arcane rites

---

21. These are technical terms. We used them every single time. Clearly, we were professionals.

were performed by John (Mr. Crockett, lately) and Julia. Julia handled nights, and looked after closing up the store. We trusted Julia to look after things, of course, but John wanted to sleep in the next morning. He'd been opening the HQCS every day for months now, so anything after 5:30 seemed like an extravagance. And since Julia had mentioned that there was a bit more water leaking that night, he thought the boiler ought to be tucked in too. Just a quick double-check.

I headed up to bed, lit some candles, and put his book on his pillow. I got out my book, and figured he'd be up before long. Only, I sort of dozed off. At 3:00 a.m. I woke up and he still wasn't there. I might have panicked. Just a bit. The stresses of the Alamo, er, store, had been weighing John down. Anything could have happened! What if he'd had a heart attack? It could happen. Stress is a killer, or so I'm told. Oh God. What if he'd fallen down in that awful cellar and hit his head? Or hit his head and fallen down . . . whichever.

Distressed, I called the store. A strange voice answered. "Yeah?"

"Uh . . . Hello. Um. This is Ellen Stimson. Is, um, John there?"

"Yep." At least I knew it was a Vermonter.

"Well, okay, listen could I . . . I mean, uh, who are you? Where is he? Is everything all right? Can I speak to him?" I'm not really sure that Phone Guy could understand me, but I do know that he didn't want to keep listening to me.

"Hang on." And then there was a considerable pause, before a beautifully familiar voice came on the line.

"Hello."

"John! Who was that? What's going on? Are you all right? It's three o'clock in the morning! Where are you?" I knew that, yes, he was at the store. He was talking on the store phone. But you have to give me a little credit for coming anywhere close to a complete sentence at that stage.

"That was one of the firemen. Greg, I think. *Wah-wah-wah-wah wah wah wah . . .*" I couldn't hear properly after he said the word "firemen." Firemen. Again?

I kept thinking that the firefighters would think that we had burned the place down for the insurance money. Which, now that I mention it, might not have been so terrible. No. No, I shook my head hard. I was just sleepy or that particular thought wouldn't have even crossed my mind.

"Wah-wah-wah-wah wah wah wah . . ." John was still talking. "I'm fine, but I've really got to go," I heard him say, finally.

"But wait—what happened?"

Too late. He was gone.

So, you know, I got dressed. I figured that whatever emergency we were facing could be handled better in clothes. And then I did my hair. One thing I knew for sure, learned over many years, was that catastrophes worked out better when my hair looked nice. And then I put on a little mascara too. Because, you know, it always helps to make an effort. By four, I had pulled up to the store.

Okay, so I actually pulled up to the bank. The store had been cordoned off. The store, the parking lot, and about a block of downtown had been blocked off by emergency vehicles. It took my eyes a while to process what they were seeing. There were those damned orange cones again. They were everywhere.[22] They stretched down the block.

It looked like . . . possibly . . . there had been a flood. Or a fast-moving glacier. Church Street was an unplanned skating rink. It was a thick sheet of ice, too, not just a thin glazing. It could have been this thick because it was well below zero out and water was still gushing into the street. From our store.

Apparently the extra leaking from the boiler had been caused by a broken Thingamagig. What you don't really expect in this sort of situation is that a little leak will result in a ruptured Thingamagig, which will cause your auto-filling boiler to dump its entire contents into your basement. And then refill.[23]

---

22. Note to self: Buy stock in orange-cone manufacturing.
23. Funniest thing. The broken Thingamagig was a cute little part that the repair guy had on his truck. Four bucks. What?! Four bucks? Four bucks.

After several hours of trying, we finally got a hold of a town Prudential Committee person. These are the responsible citizens in charge of water, and suchlike, apparently. He got right on the task of turning the water on Church Street off. You might be asking yourself why the firemen didn't do this right away. I did. But, as it turns out, they hadn't had that training yet. An all-volunteer force has a lot of responsibilities without all the time for training that you might imagine.[24] So with the intervention of the Prudential Committee, our boiler could finally stop auto-filling and then pouring into the flooded cellar before gushing out onto the street. It was quite a scene. Imagine, if you will, a '70s disaster film . . . I'm thinking *The Poseidon Adventure* . . . taking place in an old country store. Yep, that's just about it.

You can imagine just how thrilled our friends and neighbors were the next morning. They woke up with no water, and an impromptu skating rink just outside their front doors. Between the orange cones, the sun, and a healthy dose of salt, we had high hopes that downtown Dorset would be passable again by nightfall. Eli offered that we should let it stay iced. Everyone could just take

---

24. You might also wonder why we hadn't simply turned off the water to the building. Oh, well, that must have been the handle thingy I'd found on the floor some time before. I'd thrown that away. Whoopsie. Then it turned out that the wrench couldn't quite get to the shutoff either.

the day off and skate. It was Saturday, after all.

By the afternoon, the kids and I cuddled up and had jammies day, by ourselves.

John was a little worn out.

We made the cookie dough, too. Notice I said dough, not cookies. That's because I'm not sure that we actually baked anything. We snuggled in front of the fire under an old quilt, watching *Fudge* reruns. As I often do, in such situations, I knew just what to do. I had the right solution.

I ate my weight in cookie dough.

⋙ Chapter Nine ⋘

In Like a Lamb

One early-spring Sunday, John planned a family outing. He had an inspiration, and called our friends Peter and Amy Helmetag about the lambs. In my old life, I didn't know many shepherds. Maybe I just didn't make the effort. But nowadays it was a lot more common for us to make friends with farmers of many types than it might have been in the past. Our interest in lambs might be some sort of affection for the metaphors of innocence, a celebration of the end of winter, maybe, but it's also pretty likely that they are just so darned cute. I mean, have you seen a baby lamb? Even our dog-kicking minister wouldn't kick a lamb. That's over the line. At any rate, Peter and Amy's farm had produced eighty newborns that season. Eli is good friends with their son Will, so John thought it'd be a nice day out. Eli could visit with Will, and Hannah loves baby lambs. Really, who doesn't?

We pulled on our boots and headed for Pawlet, where the oldest flock of sheep in Vermont lives on the sweetest little hillside in the whole state. Many times we have pulled over and admired those sheep grazing in the wide, green grass just above the Mettowee River. It is one of Vermont's prettiest spots.

We followed the long drive and climbed out of the car to a din of *baa baa baa*ing. There were still about twenty pregnant ewes on the hillside and a couple of proud rams looking like they could run the world. Inside the barn were sixty or so mama sheep and all of their adorable little lambs. A couple of mommies had developed mastitis since the lambing and couldn't nurse, which was, as you can imagine, a problem. One of the mama sheep had given birth to triplets, and while she was snuggling them all she was also visibly relieved when the bottles came out, giving her a break at feeding time. Two ewes had died during childbirth, and with all of the other complications, there were fifteen bottle babies waiting for fresh bottle-feeding recruits. There is no finer way to spend a day in Vermont than feeding a newborn lamb its bottle.

And so we spent the day feeding lambs. I mean, really. This beautiful place and these gentle creatures could ease the most troubled heart. That was a gift we needed. Peltier's had pretty well gone from bad to catastrophic. As we tried to put out fires, we kept finding that somehow our fire hoses were all filled with gasoline. I blame the lady who drove off with our pumps.[1] But here

---

1. Okay, not really.

we were, needed and loved—for a little while—by gentle creatures and good neighbors. It was idyllic.

And can you imagine how this idyllic story turned out? We were in the car with our seat belts on, beginning the drive home, when Eli quietly muttered, "Will said I could have a lamb to raise."

We all looked at each other.

After all, we needed a little happiness in our lives right then, and maybe it made us giddy. And we *did* have a heated chicken house. Plus, we figured Eloise could probably use a little lamb to look after. There wasn't even any discussion.

We turned right instead of left and headed back up to their house. When we got out of the car, Peter asked us if we'd forgotten a lamb. These farmers and their sense of humor. Peter had particularly great timing. Before long, he had persuaded us to take two. We weren't taking these little guys permanently. They were part of the flock, of course. And, really, we weren't shepherds. At least not yet. But we could foster these little orphan lambs for a while as they were growing up. They needed special attention in these tough early days, and, of course, bottle feeding. So Peter would foster these lambs out to us and then we would bring them back sometime around June, when they could manage without the bottle. And, as he explained, when we brought the lambs back, the flock would likely not accept them immediately. They'd have each other, though, and that would make their eventual reintegration a lot easier.

So we decided to foster a little girl and a little boy. We called them Daisy and Charlie. Charlie was just a couple of days old and still a little wobbly. He was also very, very tiny. His mom had been old, and she'd died in childbirth. Daisy's mom died the same way, but Daisy was a much more mature, week-old girl. She was teaching Charlie the ropes. She had been struggling as part of the flock and really needed some individual attention. Uh-huh.

As we began to drive away, talking about what we'd need to do to get the chicken house ready, Amy suggested through an open window that if we were thinking about bringing the lambs in at night, we might want to give them a bath. Not that there was any reason to expect that we would be bringing them inside. No. No, of course not.

They went into the tub first thing.

You know, a little shea butter soap made them whiter than we'd ever imagined they could be. And, oh my, how adorable.

They played with Pippi the Moodle all around the house. She chased them, and then brave Daisy would do this little head-bent-down head butt and *baa*. Pippi backed up, lay on her back, and wriggled. Charlie would wander over, sniff Pippi's tummy, and then the whole thing would begin again. We laughed and watched for hours.

Pippi figured out the rules of the game pretty quickly, and before long she was mimicking the head butt. Such joy. Eloise curled up and indulgently let them sidle up to her warm Berner coat. Even Grandpa Stuart, Cairn Terrier Lord of the Manor, grabbed a toy and started running around like a youngster. There is nothing like a little lamb.

We did put them in the chicken house after they got their bottles. Of course we did.

For about an hour.

Then John and I went out to check on them and found them looking forlorn and lost. They weren't sleeping, but were wandering around the edges of the house. In silent agreement, we each bent down, picked one up, and aimed straight for the kitchen. Hannah and Eli were watching from the windows. The lambs curled up on the kitchen floor.

I reminded John that this was the outing he had planned.

I guess he has a softer spot for orphaned lambs than he does for wandering stray goats.

By the middle of the week, I was sitting in the sunshine watching those baby lambs race across the yard, with Pippi, our herding Moodle, fast at their heels. This had been a good plan. Charlie and Daisy galloped in big circles on the grass, playing dodge with us when it was time to come inside. But as soon as we nabbed them, they chewed on our chins and earlobes and fell asleep in our arms before we got back to the kitchen. They lay still next to the warmth of the radiator, each with the other's ear in their mouths.

We were up at 2:00 a.m. giving bottles to the lambs. For such new babies, a missed feeding with no easy mama access can spell disaster. One morning, we were just getting up for the 5:00 a.m. feeding when we heard a hysterical bleating from the kitchen.[2] I raced down, wondering what had happened, and found Charlie screaming *Baa baa meeeh meeeh . . .* which translates roughly into, "OHMYGOD I am bleeding to death!"

Charlie has a docked tail, and he had scuffed it with his hoof. The wound had reopened and scared him out of his little lambie wits. It didn't seem to hurt him, though, when I dabbed and cleaned it, coating it with Neosporin. Turned out that he was just a run-of-the-mill overreactor, like everybody else around here. He fit in nicely with our bunch.

The next night I woke up hearing the clip-clopping of little hooves. Benjamin had come by late and neglected to reattach the little gate at the kitchen. So the kids had gone exploring. I found them in the library, chewing up a purple candle.

---

2. Yes, they were still sleeping in the kitchen.

Their mouths were pinker than usual for days. They looked pretty well delighted with their adventure.

The Thursday after we brought home the lambs I had to get back on the road for some business meeting somewhere or other. There were a lot of these going on at the time and most of them required a rather involved travel schedule. Now, it had been a long time since I had had a baby. And when my babies were little I was not in the habit of feeding them and rushing off anywhere other than maybe the front yard with them in the front pack. But here we were. I raced around, filling bottles, feeding babies, cleaning poop, getting dressed, and gathering my briefcase and important papers. Naturally, I was running a little late. So when I got to my business appointment, and kept noticing the stale, sickly scent of old milk, I wasn't as surprised as you might expect. From what I could tell it was apparently on my shoulder . . . or maybe in my hair. I'm sure that Charlie could help me find it later. In the meantime, if anyone noticed, I decided to just tell them that I'd been nursing my newborn the previous night. That should shut down the pinstriped-suit crowd pretty quickly.

We go a little crazy up here in the winter. Well, more so in winter than usual, I guess. I don't remember ever wanting sheep. I still didn't want sheep, exactly. But these two sweet babes were clearly not sheep. They were our sweet dear little lambs. We delighted in the little woolly curls showing up on their spindly legs every morning. When you came into the room, you were always greeted with a sweet little *baa,* and when you gave them a bottle and they looked up at you with those milk-drunk eyes . . . oh my. That's all. Just, oh my. Their bodies would sort of snuffle and purr. I had started imagining that we better get some fencing pretty soon.

One day my Indian-food-loving oldest, Benjamin, asked what is so special about lamb, anyway, that makes people think they need to eat these dear little creatures. He said it as Charlie nuzzled his chin and fell asleep with his cheek buried at the base of his throat. So everyone was in on it. Even the college guy who had once upon a time surely loved a good lamb curry.

One day in one of our many many chase scenes, we found the little wildcats under the porch. That was when we discovered that, for lambs, satellite cable is an especial delicacy.

Benjamin declared, "We need to get a book on livestock. We just don't know enough."

"I've got the books, I just haven't had time to read them. How about you? You know," I added, "these lambs are good practice for the cow."

Eli wondered, "Could the cow please have a calf?"

I assured him, "Of course, how else will we get all the milk to make the cheese?"

John was silently beginning to wonder if that day out at the sheep farm had been a terrible, terrible mistake. For once, it really wasn't my fault.

No one would describe our house as a farm. We did not live on a farm. We lived in a high-end little picturesque village in Vermont filled with people who moved here from somewhere else. Our house even had a name, for God's sake. Does Manorside sound like a farm name to you? Most of our neighbors came from Manhattan, and more than half live here only part-time. But we do live off a little lane up a hill from the historic village center, wrapped by a forested and protected knoll, and so our chickens and critters are more or less a secret. These lambs, though, brought up some questions, because, you see, we are not farmers. Most of what I know about farming comes from the See 'n Say I had when I was about one. I know what sounds the animals make, and I know roughly what they produce.[3]

What I did not know was what it means when a lamb coughs. I didn't know the diseases of sheep, or how to treat them if I could even begin to identify them. I did not know how to mend a fence, or how to keep lambs from eating the little irises that were just then pushing their sweet little green heads up out of the cold dark earth.

---

3. Sheep = wool. Cows = milk.

When our dear friends Karen and Jack Krasny brought their little dog Madeleine for supper one night and she, excited at watching the lambs jumping, decided to chase the chickens, I knew that chasing her would only excite her more. I knew that and yet I chased her, still. So did the lambs. And screamed . . . me, not the lambs . . . and only a bit . . . it was dignified screaming. Anyway, stories of dogs chasing livestock, especially older livestock like, say, our chickens, often have very bad endings. The chickens were clucking and scared out of their wits. Madeleine was excited, and probably couldn't hear her name, let alone respond to a lie-down command. To be fair, it would have been a little hard for her to get her head wrapped around "Lie down" while Jack and I were running around the yard, yelling, in my case like a fishwife, sweating, coughing, and being chased by two frightened *baa*ing baby lambs. Finally I ran smack into Jack, who looked like he might have a heart attack at any minute. It was just another evening in the Rushing-Stimson home. Eventually, somebody nabbed the dog. The chickens flew into their house, and the lambs got bottles and a good-night rocking. All was, again, right with our little world. None of this was the dog's fault. It was the fault of the non-farmers, who should have never let a strange dog into the yard where it might be enticed to molest the livestock. That would be us, if you haven't been keeping up. This whole farm thing might not have been exactly working out, but I hadn't really caught on yet.

We didn't even have a barn. What we had was a fancy chicken house that looked like something some silly yuppies who wanted blue eggs would build.[4] Just looking at it, though, there *was* that coop out back where perhaps we could add a sheep expansion. It would cost a bundle to heat and side and insulate. And it isn't like we were just rolling in cash then, either. I hardly ever answered the phone. The store was quickly bleeding us just about to death. And on top of that, there was a fence around part of the smallholding, which was mostly just for show. It needed shoring up if it were going to contain lambs, much less sheep. We'd have to fence in the garden. Sure the lambs were only fifty bucks apiece, but owning the lambs could cost well into the thousands. And we always loved that our dogs and cat and chickens hung out with us in the yard. Would the sheep? Because at the rate they were downing their bottles they would surely be full-grown sheep rather than lambs, probably sooner rather than later.

But lambs or sheep, it couldn't be denied. We were all getting attached to one another. Soon there were going to be decisions to make.

---

4. Yep. That would be us.

Charlie could by this point jump three feet straight into the air. It was exactly like watching the Christmas Rudolph cartoon, only this was the live stage-show version. He would run sideways, kicking up his heels behind him, twisting and turning in the air like a little circus acrobat. He was the epitome of every baby animal everywhere feeling fresh and finding his legs. He was pure joy in a wool suit. The little guy could run circles around Daisy, as if to say, "Look at me, I am a RAM!" He might only have weighed five pounds, but he was destined for three hundred and he wanted everyone to know that he knew it, too.

For once, I was actually trying not to control the decision. Everybody has the right to begin and to learn something new, of course. Is that what I was aiming at? Had I secretly decided I wanted to be a farmer, even boutique-sized? Would those little guys come when we called them? Charlie already followed me around just like the Mother Goose rhyme promised he would, but would he when he weighed a hundred pounds? How about three? Who would trim their hooves? What about shearing? Is this really what we[5] wanted to be doing in our middle years? The questions kept piling up.

The baby lambs had been a surprise. It had

5. Okay, okay . . . I.

been a while since we had gotten a big surprise in this family.[6] It had come welcome and sweet, and we were glad to be fostering. But now, the next bits could be a challenge. We knew we must decide and plan, or it would surely come to a rough end. When they were curled up in front of the fire after being given their bottles and a little warm bath, they looked like an old oil painting come to life. Their black noses outlined against all that white wool and their eyes heavy with a milky sleepiness, they were an ancient kind of beautiful. They curled around one another and *baa*ed and *coo*ed each other quietly to sleep. Their beauty often took my breath away. But soon, decisions would have to be made.

We were not cut out for farming.

I had woken up to a dead baby lamb. Everyone had gone to bed after bottles and cuddles. They loved a long snuggle after their bottles. Especially Daisy.

She'd never had a mom, and she had been glad to let us substitute. She would sit in our laps with her legs curled under her for long stretches of time. She was comfortable there, until Charlie started baaing and jumping and begging her to play. She would reluctantly look up for one last

---

6. A good surprise, that is. Like a surprise party. Not a bad surprise, like "We've prepared your bill, Ms. Stimson."

cheek rub from John's beard, or one more ear scratch from me, before climbing down. She'd let Charlie chase her and play the head-butt game. She loved having a bath.

She must not have gotten any colostrum. She had all manner of little infections. She had a joint infection from a compromised umbilical cord. She had a mouth infection that forced us to encourage her to the bottle for two of our four weeks together. She was never as robust or as fully a leaping, playful lamb as Charlie. She was paper-trained. He chewed up the paper.

And that night, some little bug that any other lamb would just have fought off got her. Maybe it was bloat. This can happen when the fat in the milk replacer mixes in a hot tummy and causes a gas that cannot be expelled. She had hiccups, and then she died. It was as simple and as devastating as that.

We called Peter, and he was quite philosophical about the whole thing.

"Ellen, this little lamb almost died two or three times in her first week. She just wasn't meant to make it. It happens. Thanks for calling and telling me."

John buried her and came in with a tear-stained face.

I held a lonely and confused Charlie. Going back to the flock would be an even tougher adjustment for him now. Those sheep were wild compared to ours. The dogs at the farm were guards, not playmates. The farm humans were interested in healthy maintenance as opposed to cuddles. Charlie would be bereft. Maybe fostering these lambs had been a bad idea from the beginning. I fretted on the phone with Peter and couldn't hang up. He reminded me that he'd had many bottle babies before, but that caring for orphans was always tricky. Not all of them survived.

Then he asked me how many bottles they'd been getting. He told me to make sure Charlie got them at room temperature, not warmed up. He reminded me that they . . . he . . . Charlie . . . would nurse for a year if he was allowed, but that that would make his return to the flock even harder. Peter matter-of-factly suggested, "You know, you could cut out a bottle today, and then another on Saturday. Then he's down to one per day. More hay, more food, less attention."

Of course, I knew he was right. Peter Helmetag ran an ethical farm with much success. He has the oldest flock in Vermont. His sheep were healthy and happy and I had no idea what I had been thinking. There was a lot to be learned from this strong, kind man.

But Charlie was bonded to the dogs already, and without Daisy his affection for them would only increase.

Whose terrible idea had all this been, anyway?

Shit . . . I was not cut out to be a farmer.

●●●

Pippi went to the hairdresser the next day, so Charlie had his first full day without Daisy or Pippi in his world. Eloise was a big, loving, kindly maternal dog, but she was in no shape to play with a growing ram. Stuart, at twelve, was likewise not amused with all the head butting, charging, and jumping glee either. He was, however, always game for a walk in the woods. So when John saw the fox at the fenceline and decided to follow her, Stu and Charlie followed right alongside.

Now, we take our dogs on woodsy walks off-leash all the time. Zoe, our Bengal cat, came along more often than not. She would stick to the tree line, hopping from fallen log to fallen log, running and jumping and climbing, but never more than eight or ten feet away. She was always part of the pack. Our animals had formed a family system of their own and they traveled and acted as any pack of same-species long-bonded critters would.

Finally, Charlie was permitted into the group for the first time. He followed along at a slower pace, stopping to chew every other branch and munch on any clump of grass in his way. Stuart ran ahead, leading the little group, then John, with Zoe off to one side or the other, and Charlie pulling up the rear. A man, his dog, their cat, and a lamb, following a wandering fox. What a parade they made.

And this was our life. And it was a very good life, too, in spite of . . . well, everything.

Thus the decision was made. Few were surprised. We'd decided to keep Charlie. We had sort of acclimated ourselves to the idea of fostering. But after calls to several area shepherds, we knew that Charlie would be ostracized from the flock for at least a week, maybe more. Mama sheep would kick him away when their babies nursed. The farmer and his crew would ignore his pleas to help him be accepted into the flock more quickly. Without his buddy Daisy, he would surely be bereft. His health might suffer and his weight would drop. That was only if everything worked out. Then in mid to late summer he would go to market. Somehow we had agreed we could avoid thinking about that and consider instead only the lovely childhood he and Daisy would have with us. We wouldn't interfere in the next phase. He came from an ethical farm and we would not judge the outcome from our silly vantage point of pretend farmers. But now, without Daisy . . . We couldn't do it.

But neither could we keep Charlie as a single lamb. He was lonely and sad. These are flock animals. They'd graduated to the chicken house as the weather had gotten warmer. But now Charlie was right back in our kitchen, because we could not bear for him to sleep outside alone. One night Hannah slept next to him in her sleeping bag. One night I brought him up to our bedroom.

Another night John dragged Stuart's doggie bed[7] and a blanket beside him and slept on the floor. Charlie slept soundly so long as anyone was near. Another night, it was Eloise. Once it was Pippi. Everyone took a turn.

So John and I had taken a long drive and talked about the ethical implications of fostering this now-single lamb as opposed to all the other choices. Did we have an obligation to consider what the lamb would want if he had a vote? I remember reading a book by a fellow whose dog had unaccountably fallen for the breeding ram who was there to mate with his ewes. They had seemingly become best friends, but he wouldn't consider, for a moment, letting Darryl the ram live on his farm, no matter that he and Rose had created a rare cross-species relationship. I wondered when I read that whether humans have any moral obligation to recognize the preferences of our animals. Now here was the question right in front of us.

We had never really wished for or wanted sheep. And we were clearly, by any thoughtful estimation, not cut out for fostering. We didn't have a real barn. Our yuppie chicken house could hardly count. But we did sort of relish the idea of sheep munching in the yard next to the chickens,

---

7. It was supposed to be for Eloise. She rejected it. But it is huge, so Stuart took up one tiny corner, like a king terrier.

while the dogs napped in the sun and the humans played a little badminton. There was that mile-long walk in the woods with Stuart and Pippi, Zoe and Charlie. He'd stayed right with the group like he had been doing it all his life. But what about the garden? Charlie was a high-jumping Cheviot. I'd been told there is no fence that would keep a North Country Cheviot out of a garden. But we only really loved the basil and tomatoes. Maybe we could just do a container garden up on the balcony. We had been walking Charlie all around our smallholding every day. He seemed to be learning where he could go and where he could not. Would we be able to train sheep to stay with us like the dogs did?

Sheep. Two lambs and you can start saying sheep. And that is what we decided . . . to find another bottle baby. It would be hard in the short run to start that whole baby-nursing thing again, getting up at night and cleaning up the inevitable messes. But bottle feeding would ensure cheery domesticity. So we spent several days calling shepherds all over Vermont. Did they have any bottle babies? A ewe would be nice. And since we had to start over, a little chocolate or black one would be cute this time. We weren't going to breed them, Charlie would be neutered, so mixing breeds wouldn't matter.

We were, apparently, going to have sheep. The whole family considered names. I liked "Clarence" and "Edgar." "Franklin" was under consideration, and "Louie" was in there for a while. Somebody liked "Harry" and someone else liked "Ruben."

Sheep. We were going to have sheep. I think that meant we were going to be shepherds.

And that was how we found ourselves, one morning, heading to Rutland to meet a shepherd from Middlebury halfway.[8] She had a little black Dorset ram. Nobody had a ewe that was either a bottle baby or more than a week old. Starting over is one thing. Starting way back there was another.

Hannah came home from school and together we went to meet the new lamb. We talked to ourselves all the way there. We didn't have to take him. We'd already compromised on a girl when we found this little guy who sounded so perfect. After calling farms all over Vermont, we'd found a shepherd who was originally from Australia. She didn't dock her lambs' tails because she believed in all-natural farming. The lambs were raised on goat's milk and organic grains that she grew herself. She sounded like a well-educated yuppie hippie who had actually done it, dropped out and become a self-sustaining farmer. She sounded perfect, and so her lamb would likely be

---

8. If only everyone in this town was willing to meet us halfway. Perhaps it's just the shepherds.

perfect too. But just in case, we wanted to be ready and able to say no.

Have you ever seen a lamb with a natural tail? The tails are very long and droopy . . . and, I hesitate to say this, sort of ugly. I immediately felt guilty for not liking the orphan's tail. After all, I don't believe in circumcision, and wasn't tail docking sort of the same thing? Except with lambs and, er, not with genitals. But still, almost the same thing. The lamb was inside a travel crate, munching happily on some hay. He had been a rejected twin, and this shepherd had been keeping him in her kitchen. At about eight weeks old, he was three weeks older than Charlie and about three times his size. He looked more like a baby cow than a lamb. His tummy must have weighed forty pounds all by its sloshing, rolling, woolly self. But he was sweet. He licked our faces and snuggled right into our arms. And Charlie would grow too. You can't reject a lamb just because it is no longer tiny adorable lamb size. Can you? Well, we couldn't. Being a little bigger would be no big deal. He drank goat's milk from her goats and she'd brought some along. He could transition to milk replacer, but it might cause some stomach upset. Okeydoke. So we'd call goat farmers until we found a source. That wouldn't be a big deal either.

It shouldn't have been a big deal. I called Angela at Consider Bardwell Farm, who said no to our request. Even in spite of our Zeus relationship. Turns out that she made cheese with her goat's milk. It was quite renowned cheese, actually. So, no. Sorry, but no. Many other goat farmers said no, too. It was frustrating. The good stuff turned out to be in Brattleboro, about an hour away. Can I just tell you how many times we drove to Brattleboro for goat's milk in those next few weeks? It would have been easier to raise our own goats for the milk to feed our lambs. Which would be a terrible idea. Really. I did, at least, get that.

The lamb snuggled without a peep all the way home on Hannah's lap. What a sweetie. He was really just a big baby. He nuzzled our necks and ears. He seemed perfectly content. And then we got home.

We introduced him to Charlie outside, and they seemed perfectly fine. And then Vermont decided to have a little snow. Shocking, right? It had been seventy degrees up here, but that week we got sleet and snow. Of course we did. And from seventy, we dipped down to single digits. Sure. Why not? So we hauled them back into the kitchen, where our new pal proceeded to poop and poop and poop.[9] He was nervous, I guess. But he was bigger, and so, strangely enough, was the poop. We ran out of newspapers and cucumber-scented organic cleaner in the first hour. He ate

---

9. And did I mention poop?

constantly and, as lamb biology would have it, he pooped constantly. He'd never met a newspaper and didn't feel like it would be appropriate to poop on the first ones he came across. So, no paper training for this guy. I could say the word "poop" about a hundred more times and not begin to cover those early nights. And the *baa*ing . . . He could only sleep if we were touching him.

We put tarps down in the screened porch, and took turns sitting with the crying lamb. Charlie liked having a buddy, so he slept with his head on the lamb, but eventually even he was appalled by all the *baa*ing. He walked over to his bed and looked on imperiously, as if he'd never seen such an unmanly display.

The new lamb was also clever. This is not something you look for in an incontinent, insomniac ruminant, because his first real trick was opening doors. So you can imagine the scene. We would step out of the porch area to . . . I don't know, take a phone call . . . make a sandwich . . . bundle up sheep shit on a tarp so that our ridiculously expensive renovated New England home didn't smell like the livestock-sale barn at a rodeo for five goddamned minutes . . . and he would open the door, and then we would track him to the living room, where he would be *baa*ing on the couch. That may sound cuter than it actually was. Poop!

Eventually, the boys began eating hay together.

Charlie discovered the joys of social hay. And the new lamb became quiet. That's because one of my brood was outside with him. We did not solve Charlie's lonely problem. Instead of having one lonely crying lamb in the kitchen, we somehow had two. In the yard. It was all too much, and Charlie began sympathy *baa*ing about four every morning. This had started out as a fun fostering activity, I kept reminding myself. How did we get here? The lambs were very happy together . . . so long as one of us was with them.

The naming took awhile. Our new addition was too much a baby for many of the names we'd liked. John, unaccountably, kept trying on Spanish names. I was sticking to the old farm names. Eli liked rocker names and Hannah and Benjamin offered an eclectic mix. We are an opinionated crew, and this took some time.

The new preassembled cottage barn was delivered somewhere along the way. Because apparently, we, you know, had sheep. We were practically shepherds, and so, by God, we needed a barn. Fast.

So we got one. Or anyway, a lamb cottage. It came on a big truck with one sweet Vermonter delivering it. He had a hydraulic system to lower it into place, and then he used sort of a hydraulic jack to move it around just so. It was really pretty cute, with a green roof and a little window in front beside the door. Of course, it weighed two thousand pounds assembled, it sure wasn't going anywhere. Allen the delivery guy had all kinds of sayings as he lifted and pushed, grunted and pulled. At one point, he was trying to lean it over just enough to get some concrete shims under-neath and I heard him, with his shoulder heaving mightily into its side, his breath becoming ragged, and the jack tipping the whole thing precariously into the yard . . . "I wonder how much tip this rascal will take?"

'Bout that much, Allen. 'Bout that much.

The lambs knew immediately that it was for them. Then again, they seemed to be under the impression that everything at this address was for them. I don't think I was able to make a good case for disagreement. They climbed right in and began munching hay. And so . . . Tada! The lambs were living *outside!*

We would go out early in the mornings with bottles, and throughout the day we'd pet, nuzzle, and add hay or grain. Then at night we'd tuck them in, and not a *baa* would be heard until morning. They slept tucked over on one side, where we put their kitchen blankets atop the straw. They saw those blankets and headed right for them the first night.

Oh yeah, we are sleepy. This spot looks good.

There were a slew of stories in between, but after days of no sleep, bottling in the night, and trips to the vet, I was too exhausted to remember them. Suffice it to say that bottle lambs are exponentially harder to raise than chickens ever were. But they were amazingly cute, and when I came home and they ran across the yard to greet me and *baa* and *baa* for a cuddle, I could forget the empty cash register, the dicky electricity at the store, the town . . . hell, all of it. They settled in and, after chopping down our practically ancient rhododendrons,[10] removing ten thousand holly berries,[11] walking unendingly to relieve bloat,[12] finally settling on a name for our new boy,[13] and building a fence . . . so did we.

---

10. Lamb poison.
11. Even more lamb poison.
12. Lamb bloat, to be clear.
13. Santi.

❯❯ Chapter Ten ❮❮

Mud Season

There are these five seasons in New England: spring, summer, fall, winter, and mud. When the snows melt and the rivers start flowing again, things get plenty muddy in the valleys. Some years the blizzards come late and you don't need to haul out the Muck books until early April. But as soon as two fifty-degree days show up in a row, it's a sign that spring might be coming for real, and it is all the talk around the coffee counters of Quaint Country Stores.

During one such thaw, our friend, Irma Nagle, was singing that spring song. She and her son, Travis, had been driving along Route 30, enjoying the sun and trying their best to avoid the slippery melting ice, when they heard IT. It was a loud THWUMP! These two are seasoned Vermonters, so they knew that the sound was certainly ice falling off an overhanging tree. Luckily it hadn't hit their windshield, but these falling icicles can be real hazards. They fall off houses and onto pets . . . sometimes people. They plummet from draping trees, shattering windshields and denting car roofs. Irma figured they'd better stop and check for damage. If the ice got stuck on the ski rack, it could get a second chance at shattering a window when it slipped loose.

So they pulled over and Travis slipped out of the car to give it the once-over. A minute passed in quiet, sunshiny stillness. Then he slowly got back into the car. Irma asked, "Well, did you see what hit the car?"

"Yep," he replied.

"Well, is anything broken?"

"Nope."

Irma's boy talks like a Vermonter. Why say in forty-two words what can just as easily be conveyed in one? Irma is, unfortunately for her, from Connecticut, and though she's raised three boys here she hasn't fully adjusted.

"Well, was it ice? Did it roll off somewhere on the road?"

"Nope."

"Come on then. What was it?" she asked.

"Fish."

". . . Oh no . . ."

"Yep," he sagely replied.

And then they headed, in stoic New England fashion, to the car wash. You see, when the river ice begins to crack, the rivers start to flow, and the hawks can finally find breakfast again. The fish are big and cold and the hawks seem to drop more of them during mud season than at any other time of the year. They make a horrible noise when they hit the car. And the fish scales can be found affixed to windows and radio antennas for months afterwards.

Fish falling.

Out of the sky.

Really.

Irma and Travis went to the car wash right away. Unfortunately, bits of trout got caught in the ski rack, and somehow the car wash managed to bake them onto the roof. That car smelled like cooked fish for days. Of course, then the blizzard came and froze it all again, so the smell was gone . . . for a while. These are the odd benefits of unending winter.

Also, fish falling from the sky.

Maybe Job was from Vermont.

Yep.

Cleaning the chicken house sounds sort of disgusting. And, okay, it is. But it is also deeply satisfying. We have a flock of friendly chickens who will clamor for bits of my croissant on a spring morning when I am outside having coffee. Collecting warm, just-laid eggs from a newly cleaned little chicken house, with its fresh smell of new hay, pine shavings, and fluffy birds, is an ancient pleasure.

So there I was digging out the mess from a blasted, long winter. When we clean a chicken house, it's quite a day's work. We shovel everything out onto tarps, and shake them all over the woods on the little knoll behind our house. Those woods are so well fertilized that when spring finally comes, flowers pop up everywhere. Then we power wash all the windows and the egg boxes until everything smells clean and new. Next, we load in the first layer of piney pellets, followed by a foot or more of pine shavings. The egg boxes are filled with nests of hay and straw, and the coop outside gets a wonderfully soft layer of fresh straw to soak up the mud that April will surely bring.

It is a full day's work after a tough winter. Then there are "touch-ups" year round. I'm well and truly filthy fifteen minutes in, but at the end of the day when the girls wander around clucking at my feet, fluttering up and arranging the boxes just to their liking, the worth of it is clear. So on one early-April Saturday a year or two into our chicken-raising efforts, with the forecast for sun and the promise of morning coffee outside just around the corner, we scheduled the chicken-house cleaning.

We began with dark coffee and old jeans. We found the tarps and the rakes and the shovels and carried them round the back. We put on our gloves and had one more coffee for luck. By ten, we had been planning and rhapsodizing long enough about how nice it would be to get the work done that we figured we'd better get started. And then at eleven, the ladies started coming.

Now, you may have heard me refer to the chickens as our ladies, and that would be the case. We think of them as sort of elderly farm ladies strutting around the yard. As yet, however, the chickens haven't figured out how to drive. So when a car pulled up in front of our house, we were a little surprised to meet a totally different kind of lady. She was dressed in casual New England chic, as all ladies of a certain age in Vermont are. We stood up from the tarp and the task at hand to greet our visitor.

"Good morning" seemed like the appropriate opening gambit, but somehow inadequate for denim and chicken manure. Still, you work with what you have.

"Morning! Oh my, I didn't know you kept chickens. How lovely." She introduced herself and said that she'd known this house since she was a girl. And I probably would have wanted to sit down and offer her a cup of coffee, too, to chat about the history of our home, but given the, um, wardrobe situation, it didn't seem quite right.

"I really love what you've done to the old place. Would you mind if I just wandered in and had a look around?"

"Uh, sure, Lois. Why not?"

Our visitor was quite friendly, and by now we were muddy and covered in chicken poop. As a rule, we don't go into the house once we've started. When we are quite finished, we'll strip off our grimy clothes at the door and head straight for the shower. So, thinking her a little bit odd, we nonetheless allowed that sure she should go in and have a look. Why not? If she tried to make off with the TV, we could wrap her up in a tarp until Theron got here.

Muttering, we filled the wheelbarrow and headed back to the chicken house.

Of course, when we were again knee deep in chicken poop, another car pulled up. This time, there were three of them. They mentioned that Lois Somebody had told them how lovely our house was.

"Can we use the kitchen door, or should we go around front?"

At this stage the dogs were barking up a storm. I thought about the dirty coffee cups on the counter, and the piles of laundry I'd left in the kitchen, knowing that the kids would keep the laundry going all day if it meant being exempted from the chicken-house overhaul. By now, it was drizzling a little bit and had gotten cold. Vermont was making a mockery of the spring forecast that had lured us out. My nose was running, but as I had on chicken-poop-covered gloves, I just occasionally swiped at it with my sleeve. I was a vision. So I stood looking at these women, dressed smartly in brightly colored rain gear, and then looked down at myself.

My jeans were growing stiff with a very

particular cocktail of wet mud, chicken poop, and bits of straw. My face looked like that of a little kid with a cold whose drunken parents had ignored her for the day. So I figured, oh, what the hell, if these people were rude enough to come into my yard, amid my barking dogs, and ask to walk around my *house,* because someone who had not been up here since she was a child had told them it was pretty, then fine. Sure they could go in.

I said, "Make yourself at home. There's fresh coffee, and if you want you can change a load of laundry while you're in there."

They seemed to giggle a little nervously, but by God they walked in.

John and I stood with our mouths agape. Vermonters do "drop by," it's true. We used to think it was charming. It probably still beats the sometimes snarling, often cold anonymity of city life, but still . . . what nerve!

Just as I was mid-rant, the rain picked up, and, of course, I slipped on a patch of mud, which sent me rolling right onto the poopy blue tarp. Yes. This was why I'd gotten chickens. Lovely. I was struggling to get up, slipping, sliding, and coughing from the mucky mess. No, thank you, John. I think I can get up on my own. Just keep right on laughing, why don't you. So maybe I wasn't exactly at my best, but the laughing didn't help. Finally, I got to my feet and out of the chicken shit . . . literally, anyway . . . when yet another car pulled into our driveway.

Who was it this time? What in the hell was going on? I looked practically like a homeless person here. Couldn't a person have a little privacy, for God's sake? Had the whole town heard that I was up to my elbows in muck? Did they want to see if I'd decided to wear a gypsy skirt for chicken-house cleaning? Did someone call 911 to report a poop emergency? What?!

And then I saw her . . . the lady from the historical society. What did she want?! I was cold and muddy and miserable, and by God I had just about had it up to here with these intrusions. Was she looking for a donation? Did she have a problem with the bread at Peltier's? What?! Only then, the lightbulb went off. I vaguely remembered . . . er . . . well, something. What was it? There was some conversation with someone, was it the lady at the historical society, or maybe the theater, a couple of months back. I mean, yes, the place is steeped in history, but why was I talking to the historical society? Or was it the theater? What had they wanted? Oh, yes, she had been talking about a spring house tour. Maybe it was time to finalize that?

And then, oh God . . . I sort of remembered feeling quite flattered to have been asked. There was a fund-raiser or something. They had wanted our house for their tour. Wouldn't that be lovely?

But, of course, it was a long ways off. It wasn't until after Easter. Which was . . .

Oh. My. God.

I looked down at myself. Denim, poop, and sarcasm. This was a flattering ensemble. Then I remembered telling those nice old ladies that they could change the laundry. The laundry that included, at least in part, piles of our underwear and towels strewn across the kitchen floor. Of course, there were also the dirty dishes in the sink. Oh yes.

I looked at my poor clueless husband, to whom I had likely never said a word about any house tour.[1] I looked up the hill at the latest car to arrive. I looked back over my shoulder at the chicken house, and briefly considered hiding. It's a decent-size chicken house, maybe I could just bunk in with Minnie for a day or twelve. Maybe running deep into the woods would work out better. It was spring, so, a limited chance of hypothermia. But instead I thought of my Gram. Gram always said, "Ellen, good manners will get you through almost anything."

So I did the only real thing that I ever could do. I walked up the hill, took off my poopy gloves, offered my cold, chapped hand, and said, "Hello, won't you please come in?"

---

1. That wouldn't be unusual. It just slipped my mind. Things do that sometimes, you know.

• • •

There comes a day around here when you just have to declare that winter is over and then stick to it. This typically coincides with the beginning of daylight savings time, and after our second, particularly grim, winter at the HQCS, what a glorious beginning it was. It got up to fifty degrees here, and most of the snow melted. Oh, we still had those three-foot icy drifts against the house. Those would need chiseling, and a lot more sun, before they would go, but most of the stuff was really, finally, gone. Old ladies all over town were hammering away at the ice with rakes, shovels, and picks. It was as if someone had announced a spring-cleaning party and everyone had gotten the memo. We were all out there. Even the robins were hanging tight to the apple trees and making a glad sound.

We started picking up branches that had fallen from the trees over the winter and carrying them into the woods. I hung a little painting on the front porch, and brought out pillows for the swing and the chairs. We took away the winter locks that tighten the doors, keeping the wind at bay, and then threw them open. The dogs loved it. They ran out into the mud, following the rivulets of water all over the meadow. We had tiny streams and itty-bitty rivers all over the place. Eloise and Stuart were certainly going to need a bath, but they deserved it. Winter might be tough for a Bernese Mountain Dog, but for a Cairn Terrier it lasts an age. Let them roll in the mud.

I put away everything in the house that even hinted at winter. There were birch branches in vases covered with little pink and red felt hearts left over from Valentine's Day. I put away the old French glass pinecones and replaced them with German Easter eggs. A couple of spring-like iron rabbits hopped out onto the sideboard, and I put fresh pastel-colored candles out to replace the red tapers that had burned since February.

We're a flag family. Not necessarily the Stars and Stripes, though that's certainly right around Independence Day, but rather we hang seasonal flags. So I pulled down the snowman that had been flying for quite some time now, and replaced him with a banner covered in irises. I had declared that it was spring. I would even fly the flag.

After emptying the old dead potted plants that had been sitting on the porch throughout the darker days of winter, we lingered on the porch till the sun went down. It was at least 6:30. That's 6:30 p.m. It was well and truly spring.

Of course, the next day the schools were on snow delay. Overnight, the skies decided to protest my little flag-waving declaration. Sure, I'd made a stand. So had the cold front moving through New England. The roads were icy and the porches were covered in a thick white blanket. This is what the locals call a sugaring snow. Big wet flakes fell overnight, but we'd see higher temperatures again tomorrow. Folks would be out tapping trees and boiling sap.

It was, apparently, that time of year. There would be low temperatures at night, a few wet snows, and then sunny, warm days, which would mean thick, rich maple syrup. I love to go into the sugar shacks to breathe in the hot, syrupy smells. Each farmer creates a syrup with his own signature taste. His particular maples yield a certain type of sap, and he keeps his fires at just the right level to generate the perfect consistency.

Each syrup is graded from Fancy down to good old B. Vermonters tend to prefer the dark, rich B-grade syrups. Fancy and Grade A are a thin, lightly flavored syrup. But for the true Vermonter, pale amber syrup just isn't going to do. Nosiree. Vermonters are real B people. And, I suppose, so are we now. We like that dark, thick sugar. It's not heavy like molasses is, but it is much richer than the syrups you'll find in a diner. And it has a deep maple flavor that lingers.

So, it looked like winter again out there. The purple, orange, and blue glass eggs we'd laid out inside seemed a little premature. But, you know, that was okay. We'd had a taste of spring. And this . . . this was just a little snow. It wouldn't amount to much. By the next day, it would be part of the flowing streams that were rolling down the mountains. The mud from those streams would roll down, rich with nutrients, and lay the foundation for all that color that we looked forward to in the fall. It was snowing now, and we'd need a fire today. But finally, it was spring in Vermont.

Of course, the next day, school got canceled for mud. They called it a headmasters' holiday but everyone knew what it really was. We were all knee deep in, and sick and tired of, mud. Our friends Karen and Jack live just five minutes away, but they are up high on Rupert Mountain, so it is a key five minutes. They get about six more weeks of winter up there than we do down here in the valley. I called Karen, and sure enough she was mudded in. Snowed in? Everyone everywhere has heard of being snowed in. But mudded in? Only in Vermont. Half of this state lives on a dirt road, and the school buses just couldn't get through after three long days of pounding rain. In Vermont, the snow runs off the sides of the mountains after a long winter, and since most of the people actually live in valleys, we get buried. In America's North Country, spring comes in the form of rain. That rain comes on top of snow softening the drifts and melting the ice. Walking across the snow opens up the hard, bare ground beneath it with every step. You know that something is happening underneath all that snow because you can hear the water running underneath. Before long there are the squishy sounds of your boots as they ease across the yard, which complements the constant sound of running water. There seems to be a whole separate world just below the snowy, melty surface. The earth is waking up, and the birds are coming back.

There had been heavy snows and quick melts. Ice, snow, and rain had blanketed us. Through it all, the deer still walked the same trails they had been maintaining all winter. They mashed the snow into hard-packed rough ice-coated mud clumps that would remain long after the softer snow melted away. Their footprints had become the icy understory in the forest. We throw hay and salt down in the meadow for them as winter ends. They'd already gotten all the low bark off our trees. The coyotes take more of them in the late-night hours. It sounded like a horror movie out there some nights. When we can stand it no more, we start throwing hay. The locals chastise us for this, of course. Vermonters let nature take its course. And I try. I really do, but by March I feel like everyone needs a little Disney break, so I cave in. I fatten up a few deer and the coyotes move on to somebody else's woods.[2]

Our smallholding backs up to a protected forest trail. So we have wild woods that begin just at the edge of our land. Our chickens don't lay well when the coyotes are hunting in our meadow. The sounds that interrupt our sleep seem to unsettle

2. A salt lick really draws them in.

the hens as well. And we don't need wild animals molesting our livestock, so we fatten up our Kent Hill deer. They are faster and stronger, so the coyotes move on.

The signs were everywhere. The sleepy season was almost over. The late-winter farmer's market in Brattleboro that Saturday was filled with cute little girls in dresses and boots. Their Vermont mamas were selling a winter's worth of pottery, their long braids tied back in flowery ribbons. There was Thai food and live music. All the farmers had little pots of veggies and flowers for your house. They offered piles of seeds filled with hope and promise. Trapped in our own houses through the winter, we'd missed each other, even those of us who might have been destroying a Quaint Country Store. The sunny Saturday market was cause for celebration. We came right home and ordered new baby chicks.

That Sunday, we went out to the pond and saw that the geese were coming back, too. The first ones were just arriving, hanging around the edges of the pond and grabbing the fish that were swimming up to the surface, enjoying the sunshine. Or anyway, enjoying it right up until they met the geese, but still. The first geese of the year are huge. It's as if the strongest sentries arrive first. They make a big racket, trumpeting the sound of spring. Welcome back, guys. Watch out for the mud.

⋙ Chapter Eleven ⋘

The Alamo

I am not an organized person. I lose my keys. All the time. I am one of those people who has to call her phone to find it. And I am the kind of person who might forget to get the car inspected. But, aren't we all? From time to time. Of course, not getting the car inspected delays getting the new license plates. But really, aren't the old ones just fine? Well, no, as it turns out.

We were deep in the dark, final days of the Horrible Quaint Country Store. I had, of course, forgotten the inspection. I couldn't then get an appointment that worked for my schedule, and so I missed getting the new plates in time. Meanwhile, I got the tiniest little speeding ticket in New York State, that I also might have forgotten to pay. We were out of checks, for one thing, and you couldn't pay by credit card. So I put the ticket on the bulletin board at home as a reminder to order the checks, and who knows what happened to it after that?

Did you know that your driver's license expires on your birthday in Vermont? I found that out when I got the ticket in New York; but the nice young officer, who was certainly no older than twelve, didn't notice. So I didn't tell him. I promised myself that I would take care of it as soon as I got back to Vermont. Only, I couldn't. Because, of course, you can't take the driving test without current plates, which you can't get without an inspection. See! They were just making me break the law. It almost wasn't my fault.

Then, as these things happen, the car insurance renewal came up, only . . . well, you get the idea. So things were getting pretty desperate around here, as I was driving to New York every week for work.[1]

Finally, one Monday when I wasn't leaving town, I planned to run around and get the inspection, my license, and possibly a partridge in a pear tree. Only, John called me from the store first thing and asked if I could take the weekend deposits to the bank. Both of his morning people had called in sick and he was alone at the Horrible Quaint Country Store. Our banker,[2] who had been helping us through the quagmire of the store, was in Rutland, Vermont. So I figured I'd just drive up there early and do the drive-through when it opened at eight. And so at around seven, I added

---

1. Work being the businesses I was starting, it should be said, to save us from the collapsing business we'd bought in our lovely new home. Did I mention that it's beautiful here? Well, it is. And apparently there are no expiration dates on that.
2. A saint.

a heavy robe over my flannel nightgown and carried my cup of coffee to the car. Why get dressed when I was only going through a drive-through and it was too early to have to worry about seeing anyone?[3]

And it was totally fine. You can easily make a deposit through the drive-through at the bank. And, you know what, I bet the tellers at that bank have seen much stranger things first thing in the morning. It was a nice robe, after all.

I was headed back home from the bank when sirens and flashing lights suddenly made my heart race. I hadn't been speeding. Really. Pinky swear. Not this time anyway. Whatever could this state trooper want? Turns out, it seemed he had been driving, in the other direction, and spied, from way across the highway, my green inspection sticker whose color indicated its expiration.

Oh goody.

And, my driver's license had expired.

Oh, and New York had ordered my license suspended for nonpayment of their ticket.

I learned all of this as I was on the phone to my husband. The trooper suggested I keep him on the phone. Like *he* could do anything to help me? He was alone at the stupid store, where everybody in town already hated us for, among

---

3. Okay, so I'll admit to the possibility that the Horrible Quaint Country Store might have muddled my thinking just a bit.

other things, the missing necessities on the shelves. A CLOSED sign hanging out front would just double-seal our already firmly sealed fate.[4] So I hung up the phone and looked at the trooper. He looked back at me. I started imagining the mug shot in the paper of me in my nightgown. Finally, it was just all too much.

Amazingly, I didn't cry.

I said, "Now you listen here, I own the Horrible Quaint Country Store in Dorset, Vermont, and it is failing miserably; and the whole town hated us for buying it in the first place; and now we've run it into the ground and they really hate us; and I ran to the bank in Rutland to make a deposit so we wouldn't bounce any checks, because we have hardly any money in our deposit account and our credit has all been used up; and if you are thinking about taking me to jail you just need to have another think, because I am in my nightgown and my hair looks like hell; and I cannot face having my picture in the paper, so you are just going to have to figure something else out!"

I said this all in one breath and maybe just a little bit loudly. I was having the teensiest, rather small, actually, hardly worth mentioning, really, little breakdown. And the trooper must have known it. Because he said, just like any self-respecting Vermonter would, "Aye-up."

---

4. Injury, meet insult.

And then, "How about if I give you a ticket for driving on a suspended license, and you get your car inspected and try to get this mess sorted out; and when you plead not guilty, I won't show up and today will be like it never happened."

So then I cried.

I said I loved Vermont. I said he was a wonderful man. I said I would have him and his wife over for dinner. I said I was not always quite this incompetent. I sat up straighter, sniffled a bit, and smoothed my hair.

Only then he said, " 'Course, I can't let you drive home, ma'am."

So I asked him how in the HELL did he think I was going to get there? I was in MY NIGHT-GOWN, for God's sake. My husband was alone at the store. WHAT was the matter with him, anyway?

He offered that maybe we should get a cup of coffee. Which we did. It's not every morning that I wear my robe to coffee with a police officer in a gas station. Eventually, with the help of caffeine and calming breaths, I decided to call Hannah at her high school. Hannah, my organized child who was never even late with a homework assignment, didn't say one reproachful word. She just came, right away. She retrieved me from the gas station, and we left the car where it was. John and Benjamin came back for it later.

Do you know that the next day, the trooper

came into the store and asked how I was doing? He bought breakfast, too. Eventually, I did get the ticket paid and my license renewed and the car inspected and the insurance bought. The new plates shined on the back of my car.

And that trooper? He did just what he said he would do. I was found "not guilty" for driving on a suspended license. In addition to the mountains and all the stars and the sweet smell of wood smoke and the sparkly winters, I think Vermont deserves to be known for its kindly state troopers. Because my trooper brought his trooper buddies to the store, where they all bought coffee and doughnuts. They didn't say much, but they smiled and they kept coming until the very end. They often patted us on the back, and I will remember them forever.

One day, while I was in a meeting, I got an email from Davy (John) at the Alamo, the Horrible Quaint Country Store formerly known as Peltier's. The subject line said simply "Peltier's Last Day."

Now, at this stage, I read dire declarations every day about my little HQCS. Bank letters were foreboding. Tax letters were portentous. Vendor letters were menacing. Even the customer notes were baleful.

But this one stood out. It managed to sound ominous even in terrible company.

I was in New York City trying to launch one of

the new businesses I had started. I'd started three in short order. There was a little marketing company, which had investors, so that had me flying all around the country. I had a nonprofit development agency, and I was also trying to put something together in the book business, again. So my days were full. And my John, the very solid, steady guy I married, who is also one of the quietest, most private people on this earth, was back at the HQCS trying to hold it all together long enough for something to work.

This had apparently been a bad day for him. The Coke guy had come to take away the Coke cooler, since we couldn't pay our bill. John had talked long enough and sweetly enough and had somehow found just enough money to keep the Coke flowing, but he'd had it. It was all just too much.

Once, years ago, we had tried to keep an aquarium. That's an easy enough thing, right? A sweet, glowing tank of water and happiness. Only we weren't very good at that either, and our fish kept dying. Now here we were again. Owning Peltier's was like owning a very public aquarium right in the middle of town, where a new fish died every single day. The villagers[5] would drop by just to see which one was floating. That wouldn't

---

5. I never said that they had torches and pitchforks. That was never said.

have been so terrible if only they'd bought a Take Home Supper while they gawked.

By the time John wrote that email he was at the "to hell with it" stage. You know, he really didn't want a Coke cooler anymore. And if that one was gone, they should probably take the Pepsi cooler too, since by God he'd always hated Pepsi. He decided that he didn't want gas pumps either, now that you mention it. He was sick to death of those finicky gas pumps, the high price of oil, never having enough gas in the tanks, and the smell. That smell could get stuck on your hands and in your nose for days. Besides, there was always someone parked at an odd crooked angle in the too-tight space while they gassed up, so that another car waited impatiently to pull up to the store. The waiting driver was generally irritable by the time he actually got into the store. And the poorly parked gas customer felt the impatient ire from the waiting driver, so by the time he paid for his gas, he was aggravated, too. The guy behind the counter, let's just call him "John" for the sake of discussion, caught all that moodiness. So he was sick to death of the gas.

Come to think of it, he didn't want to make crab cakes on Thursday nights either. That was another smell he could do without. And while we were at it, he didn't want a wine room. Hell, he'd never wanted a wine room. He was an ale man, for God's sakes.

The thing was, he didn't want to own a fucking store anymore, much less this one. And not for one more goddamn minute.

These were the things he implied when I called.

Only, perhaps a little more colorfully.

I had been in a meeting with a bunch of gray-pinstripe-clad bankers. I'd made some excuses, run out, and called to say, "Wait, whoa. Hold on, honey. This cannot be that day."

God.

Please.

Imagine trying to sell that monster if it was just a closed, shuttered building. That would be tough enough, but we personally guaranteed the loan. The bank could, theoretically, call us for bad faith, and then the clock on the inevitable lawsuits would begin. Our house was the pocket-book for the store, and we had started borrowing against it, too, now.

What a mess. But it would be a much worse mess if we lost the house, too.

Shit.

Buck up!

This is not the time to have a nervous break-down.

All of which I was just about to say. It was right there on the tip of the tongue ready for launch, only I didn't say any of that. I was about to say it—all of it. I mean, I moved to Vermont, too. I wanted to see some stars, not goddamned pollution and concrete. I was supposed to be homeschooling my kid, not sitting in a window-less, air-conditioned room with a bunch of god-forsaken Polo-cologne-wearing bankers, checking their BlackBerrys like maybe they were in charge of the nuclear launch codes, so couldn't be bothered with an actual conversation in person. Okay, so maybe John had not wanted to buy a country store,[6] but I did not hear him coming up with any great ideas about making a living in Vermont back when we'd bought it. Maybe I did make a series of bad decisions, but someone had to make the decisions and they couldn't all be good ones, damnit. My life was not exactly picnics beside mountain streams just at the moment, either!

Only then my mild-manned John, the one who warmed up my car every single morning all winter long, the guy who let me put my cold feet next to his warm ones in bed, the man who brought coffee out to me when I had to leave for New York at 4:00 a.m., the man who danced with our babies, the fellow who ran interference with my crazy family for twenty-five years, the guy I would choose always to spend any open time with because he made me laugh every single day, that guy, said in a voice that was sort of a plaintive

---

6. Sure, now he says this!

wail, "But Ellen, you can sell *anything,* can't you please just sell *this??!!*"

I promised I'd call a realtor and we would sell the goddamn store.

He agreed to leave the door open for just a little longer. At least for today.

But the clock was running. I had to hurry, and I knew it.

I started calling everyone I knew and telling them we wanted to sell the store—cheap. I started with our friend John Sobel.

John knew everyone. He golfed when it was warm and he skied when it was cold. On a good day in spring, if he timed it just right, he could do both, and he'd have a nice sociable lunch in between. John was one of those guys who kept a good tan going until somewhere in January. I figured he could get the word out better than just about anybody.

Then I started calling realtors. I didn't sign up with any of them, but just got the gossip out that Peltier's might be for sale. And could they please keep it to themselves. In Dorset, the fastest way to spread news is to say it's a secret. By the following Monday, my manicurist was asking me about the sale.

There was a local real estate investor who had an idea for the store and wanted to help out. He and I chatted while he started quietly looking for someone to run the place. Plus, he had an in-house realtor. Would I use him? You bet.

We had two families who were interested in buying the store and putting a restaurant inside. The real estate guy was thinking maybe he'd hold the paper. The problem was that the offers were so low we couldn't begin to cover the bank, much less the original owners, who had also taken back some of the loan on our deal. There were a couple of other interested people who came and looked, as well. It felt a little like there were more people interested in buying a failing country store than there were customers interested in buying bread and crab cakes. Every time a new potential buyer called, I would start baking fresh bread in the oven and piping a little Van Morrison, or Chet Baker, over the speakers. John would put on his apron. We wanted to look like people in the middle of the Vermont dream.

We were in the middle of it all right. We were dying to wake up.

Like business deals everywhere, nothing much came of any of it. Each offer fell apart in its own way and in its own time.

Finally, a real buyer popped up. This was a local Dorset woman and her New Yorker partner. These women knew the town and the store intimately. They made us an offer. Of course, the offer was about half of what we had paid for the store. It was about two hundred thousand under our appraisal on the building alone. It was, even after all of our incompetence, a bargain. But we would still be way upside down with the bank.

And then . . . and I'm not sure how this happened even now . . . friends came forward and offered to help. Who does that? People who love you do. It was one of the most humbling times of my life.

But there was still the matter of the original owners. Many pieces had to fall in line to make this deal happen. So we made them a cash-value offer. They declined.

That was a showstopper.

By now, to say that John was fed up was a gross understatement. He was barely putting one foot in front of the other. His sense of humor was weary. He was exhausted and spent. As a girl with a wide emotional range, I was exercising all of it. I was not quite shrill. I don't think I was shrill. Not shrill, per se. But I may have been just an ever so little bit screechy. I was at the end of my rope.

We had to sell this store.

So I called David Silver.

David is a funny, warm, criminal defense lawyer. He has a bad habit of representing people who can't pay him. I was about to join the party. When you drive by David's house, his yard is always filled with almost-but-not-quite criminals fixing porches or mowing the grass. Restaurant owners who may have had a little trouble with a DUI feed him for free. He has a string of impressive wins, and everyone knows a story about someone David has saved. If you get pulled over doing anything you might not supposed to be doing, David is the guy you call. Every teenager for two counties carries his mobile number in their wallets. The doc he got off of a murder charge is a legendary story. A few years earlier, David had been part of a beefcake calendar fundraiser that had featured local guys. So Mr. July was also cute. He had a very nice smile, which made law-abiding folks not hate him too much when he was representing a child molester.[7]

Now, David is not a business lawyer. All that free legal work he does is testimony to the lack of business classes he took in college. But he is my friend. My dear friend. That turned out to be plenty good enough.

I called David's cell phone and asked him if he would call the former owners, or at least their lawyer. Could he explain what a good deal the cash offer was? I figured this would sound better coming from a lawyer, any lawyer, than from me, the woman who had brought ruin upon "their" store. They might not be inclined to hear what I had to say.

"Okay, so David, you'll want to tell them that

---

7. It might be important to note at this point that we aren't all a bunch of drunken, murdering child molesters up here. But if you happen to be, David is your guy.

cash now, at a discount, presumably for about the same amount as they could earn in interest over the life of the loan, is a good deal. It is an *especially* good deal when it's contrasted with the ten cents on the dollar they might get in a bankruptcy."

I went through a cash-value offer point by point with David, explaining all of the details. David got it. He was on vacation, but he agreed to make the call.

David explained things to their lawyer. They made a counteroffer.

He called me all happy sounding and feeling triumphant about having gotten a counteroffer. For him, it was kind of like when the state's attorney offers a plea with no jail time, right?

Poor David. This was not his regular milieu.

What I said: "Unfortunately, David, we have a finite amount of money to make this deal happen,"
Translation: *David, maybe I wasn't clear. Look, we have run out. Out. Of. Money!*

What I said: "So, there is no room to negotiate. They need either to agree, or to risk taking their chances in a bankruptcy. In a bankruptcy, the bank will come first."
Translation: *Ask them if they know how bankruptcy works. The bank will sell it off at*

an auction, take its share, and there will be nothing left. Maybe they will get a few pennies on the dollar. No kidding. What don't they get here???

I was not bluffing. My husband had had it, and so had I. We were up against the wall here. David understood. So he called them again . . . from his vacation. He was on his family vacation. His loyal friendship was humbling.

And in an hour or so, he called me back. They had made another offer. This offer was for less than before, but still more than we had on the table. David carefully, in a bit of a halting voice, wondered, "Does this one sound good to you?"

After all, David was used to negotiating when he talked to other lawyers, and negotiations mean a give and take. He might have tried to helpfully explain this to me.

I, however, was very, very . . . quiet. It felt like a dangerous quiet.

While I had been waiting for David to call back, I called our bank and had gotten the name of a bankruptcy lawyer. I explained where we were in this situation. Tom[8] was very sweet. He spoke softly, and gave me the name of a good lawyer. He may have said he was praying for us. I figured that was probably not a good sign.

---

8. The "workout" guy. Remember him?

So I made a phone appointment with the bankruptcy lawyer for two o'clock. We here at the HQCS were craving a little finality. I wasn't sure how it was going to go, but that day, for an hour or two, I was prepared for anything.

My good friend, the other Jack,[9] had been telling me for weeks, "Bankruptcy, Ellen. This is why it exists. You have a failed business. There is a mechanism for this. Bankruptcy is part of the system."

For weeks I had mulled that.

One morning he called me, just checking in. This dear sweet man who hated the phone seemed to understand just what I was feeling.

"Hi, Ellen. You still alive over there? Look, there is no shame in bankruptcy. We have whole states that are probably going to file for it. Many fine businesses have done it, and gone on to become healthier, better businesses afterwards."

But John and I just hadn't quite been able to face that. Sure, if we went into bankruptcy Coke and Pepsi would survive. So what, if we didn't pay our bills with them? But Wilcox Ice Cream was family run. They'd brought us ice cream even though we could hardly ever pay for it. And our bread guy, him, too. These were little businesses that had kept us alive. We owed them, and they deserved to be paid.

---

9. Jack Krasny.

Then there was our bank. Tom had become, practically, our best friend. He had let the overdrafts continue because he believed me when I told him that I would pay him back—he believed in me, and in some deeply moral sense I owed him.

But now, at the eleventh hour, we had one pretty crummy deal that depended on a separate cash-value deal with the previous storeowners. Without that cash deal, all of our intentions would be moot. We'd had our shoulders to the wheel, and we'd done the best we could. It had to be faced. I called Tom our banker to let him know where we were and one last time he said he was there for me.

I softly explained to David, our not-vacationing vacationing friend, what I'd done, and asked if he could possibly call the other lawyer one last time.[10]

What I said: "David, please tell them that I completely understood and sympathized with their position."
Translation: *Are they out of their minds!!!?*

What I said: "It is hard to accept that things have changed. It would be best if they consider the merits of the new offer in

---

10. David might say that I underrepresent his vast negotiating skills here. It's possible. He could be right.

light of the reality of the new landscape."
Translation: *Have they not noticed that the store is empty? There are no paper towels, no soup. No customers!!! Does 'out of money' mean anything to them? Does their lawyer speak English?*

What I said: "Cash-value deals are really common, and this one is fair. They might want to get their accountant's opinion. Sadly, they only have until two o'clock to decide.
Translation: *Cash. Value. This is basic math.*

What I said: "We've already done our deciding. Now they need to do theirs. After two, they will have to take their chances."
Translation: *Two o'clock. I am not kidding. By two, there will be a CLOSED sign on the door. We can give 'em a bottle of old balsamic, if they'd like. There's still plenty of that.*

All this "negotiating," or whatever it was that we were doing, might have seemed a little harsh to David . . . and to the previous storeowners . . . but they mightn't have understood the urgency of the situation. Because, unless we made this deal now, this really would be Peltier's last day. We had decided. This was the end of this particular road for us. We were done.

So there was a wee bit of drama, and our poor

David never did get to the beach that day. In the end, they took the deal, and John opened Peltier's the next morning with Bill and Bruce having coffee just like always.

In the Disney version, the story would end right here. Maybe the camera would zoom in on the two of us having coffee with Bill and Bruce. But this was more of a made-for-TV affair than a family-friendly big-budget Disney experience. There were still hills to climb.

A significant deal point for us with the new buyers was a June 30th fast closing, which was only about a month from when we'd signed the letter of intent. Cheap, sure, but in exchange for that price tag the buyers had to close the deal fast. We were on a clock here. When I say that we had had it there was never anything I had meant more.

Unfortunately, the buyers had the trip of a lifetime planned. It was an African safari. You know, lions and tigers and giraffes, oh my. Their realtor explained to us that "Perhaps the closing will need to be postponed."

Postponed.

Oh, and apparently the prospective owners only wanted to buy the Horrible Quaint Country Store if we kept it open during the transition.

We.

Open.

"We," as you might guess, meant "John."

So, you know . . . Uh-uh.

This was a deal breaker. This sale would not be happening.

We had hung a big calendar on the wall in our kitchen. We were literally counting down the days. John was just hanging on. The store shelves were barren, our customers were all mad, our banker was sending us little notes of encouragement, our kids were scared, our vendors were praying for us when they weren't threatening us, even the dogs looked morose. Everyone had had it.

The buyers' realtor didn't understand. I'm sure he must have figured that since we had no choice but to sell, I would come around.

He and I had only recently met.

He didn't know me very well.

There had been another potential buyer a few months earlier who came suddenly to mind. Jack DeSario was another lovely Dorset guy who had a couple of successful restaurants in New York.[11] I had gotten to know him a little since he had moved onto our street. John and I both liked him a lot. For one thing, Jack had a well-loved Bernese Mountain Dog named Otto. Our Eloise loved his Otto. Additionally, he had a laid-back, cheerful air of success. He seemed smart. He'd wanted to open a restaurant in Dorset, and he had considered the store earlier, when the price tag had been higher.

---

11. I have had a lot of good luck with the Jacks in my life.

So I called him up. I explained in one really long run-on sentence with no breaths exactly what was happening. By now everyone knew how tough things were. I explained about the letter of intent we'd signed that had stipulated a June 30th closing, and how the realtor was talking about another month, which might not seem to be a lot unless you were well and truly at the end of your rope. And then . . . well then it just was.

I told him what the current price of the store was. Then I wondered out loud about whether, if the letter of intent were compromised and the deal fell through, he just might be interested in the store.

"Are you sure? Wow. What a bargain. Give me an hour to think it over."

Jack called back in twenty minutes. He'd get me an offer in writing, and a good-faith deposit, in a couple of hours. I explained that I would have to call the original buyers' realtor and tell him what was happening.

He understood, but added, "El, wait till you have my check in hand, then call him. If they want to stick to the agreement closing in thirty days, no harm, no foul. I'll open my restaurant somewhere else. If they don't, hell, then I guess I'll own that little quaint country store of yours."

I did a hallelujah dance for Saint Jack.

The realtor was apoplectic.

"But you signed a *Letter. Of. Intent!*"

He said it like maybe it was the Declaration of Independence.

I agreed that "Yes, we did. With a June thirtieth closing."

"A closing change doesn't violate the letter," he asserted.

"Really?" I asked. "Huh. Gosh, I think maybe it does. Anyway, we need an agreement to close the sale by June thirtieth. And if you are planning on agreeing to that and then backing out, we'll get to close it anyway. You still have to buy it, or be in contract violation. That violation would cost you a fat daily fine. Or, if you prefer, we can just sell it to this nice guy who'll close on our date. And, you know, now that I think about it, he doesn't have a realtor. So we'll save that money, too. Huh, in fact, maybe we should just—"

"I'll call you right back."

And he did. June 30th turned out to be fine after all. What do you know?

Bless Jack DeSario's good heart. Bless his heart.

We weren't in town for the closing. The five of us went to the Northeast Kingdom. Lake Willoughby, in northeastern Vermont, is a natural wonder. It is a glacial lake with two mountains rising up behind it, creating an Arctic Alpine vibe. Surrounded on all sides by mountains and forest, it is utterly pure, clear, and absolutely gorgeous. There are about a million pine trees lining the shores, so the piney smell is the first thing you notice when you step out of your car. It is profoundly quiet and wild.

We rented a big, cheap pontoon boat and sailed to Canada and back on the day of the closing. We jumped off the side of the boat and swam in another country.

That night, we made a bonfire outside our cabin. We roasted hot dogs and marshmallows under the cope of stars next to a big, beautiful blue lake shimmering beneath a full shiny moon. It seemed like a good omen.

We held hands, got into canoes, and counted shooting stars. I saw one on the first night and started to make a wish. For a second, I couldn't quite think what to wish for. John said he didn't need one since his wish had already come true.

I looked around.

We'd brought the dogs with us, and they were stretched out on the shore full of, ironically, hot dogs. The family was all here . . . together. Maybe my wish had already come true, too.

Eli was the only one of us who was a little sad that day. Peltier's had been his confectionary. He had all the soda and chips he and his pal, Timmy, could eat.

"I don't see why we couldn't have kept it," he complained. "Won't you guys miss the candy counter?"

"No, honey. Actually, we won't. But don't

worry, we'll go to the Vermont Country Store whenever you want . . ."

That night, with our fingers sticky from s'mores, we told happy ghost stories. None of them involved haunted country stores.

Grateful and exhausted, I got a little teary. I just couldn't hold it all together for one more minute.

Hannah, a tall, elegant high schooler now, was holding our hands just like she had when she was little. She looked at her dad and then back at me and said, "Don't worry, Mommy, everyone makes mistakes."

Then right away Benjamin said, "We'll get it back. All the best success stories have some horrible tragedy stuck right smack in the middle."

John reached over and gave my shoulder a squeeze.

"No more stores though, okay? Let's promise—no more stores."

With all the windows open and the smell of pine and marshmallows all around us and the sounds of crickets and settling trees, we dragged the mattresses off the beds and snuggled under our big down quilts in front of the fire.

Pretty soon we would have to go back home. There would still be stuff to face, but not tonight. Tonight, we drifted off to sleep in that big woodsy cabin, once again all together. This might have been worth wishing for.

❯❯ After Words ❮❮

I like food. Okay, that doesn't completely cover it. I love food. I love cooking it, eating it, and talking about it. I love everything about it. I especially like finding the perfect ingredients and preparing a long, happy meal, and sharing it over funny stories with family and friends. Lots of my food has a story to go along with it, and lots of my stories have some food to go along with them, too.

These next bits are not exactly the kinds of recipes you might expect to find in a cookbook. I am not someone, for example, who measures. I am more of an estimator. This is how I cook and how we eat. You won't always find which size saucepan to use or any directions about boiling and peeling. You might, however, find some good ideas for supper.

CHEESE

And cheese. Let me count the ways. Around here, you'll find a fabulous boutique dairy every few miles along the road, just like the one where Zeus lives. Some of these dairies sell their milk and cheese just inside the barn, on the honor system. There is usually a refrigerator with a hand-lettered sign and a cash box. You make your own change. Then you write what you took on the clipboard hanging from the ceiling. You might pay a deposit on your jar of milk. Next week you bring your jar back, so you only have to pay the deposit once.

It is quaint, charming, delicious, and well-nigh irresistible. So I had to come up with a whole bunch of new recipes to use all the cheese that suddenly found its way into my home.

Vermont Mac 'n Cheese
This one will not make you skinny, but it will make you happy.

About a pound of macaroni
A couple of tablespoons of olive oil
4 ounces thick cured bacon, preferably from
  local happy pigs
5 cups whole milk, preferably raw

¼ cup sweet butter

About ½ cup flour

About 1 cup grated hard cheese (I like a local Parmesan when I can get it. Aged two years, if available.)

1½ cups grated Gruyère (Sheep or goat is especially lovely here in the mountains. Older cheeses have that wonderful nutty flavor.)

1½ cups grated Vermont sharp cheddar (How sharp? Really sharp . . . and from cow's milk.)

1½ teaspoons good salt (less or more to taste)

½ teaspoon fresh ground pepper

½ teaspoon nutmeg

Preheat the oven to 400°F.

Cook the macaroni al dente in salty water. Drain, toss with the olive oil, and set aside in a large mixing bowl.

Add the bacon to a small skillet and sauté over medium heat until brown, but not crisp, about 10 minutes. Drain, then add to the cooked macaroni.

In a medium saucepan, bring the milk just to a foamy boil, then reduce the heat to very low.

In another saucepan, melt the butter over medium heat. When the foam subsides, remove from the heat. Whisk in the flour and continue stirring until a smooth, pale roux has formed. Return the saucepan to medium heat and, while whisking steadily, begin ladling the hot milk into the roux, 1 cup at a time, completely incorporating each cup before adding the next. After all the milk has been added, continue to whisk until the sauce thickens and bubbles gently, about 2 minutes. Add the hard cheese, half the Gruyère, and all of the cheddar, along with the salt and pepper and nutmeg. Stir until the cheese has completely melted.

Pour the sauce over the macaroni, mix thoroughly, and pour into a buttered 10-by-14-inch gratin dish. Back in the oven for 12 minutes. Remove, sprinkle the remaining cup of Gruyère over the top, and continue baking for an additional 10 minutes until the top is golden and crunchy.

Panzanella

Here's one to use with your blue cheese. It is marginally healthier than the last one.

Baguette . . . crusty and fresh
1–2 tablespoons olive oil, depending on how big your baguette is
Garlic cloves, crushed for rubbing
Salt and pepper to taste
Arugula (you know, enough for a salad for two plus a little more)
Mixed greens (about half of one of those bags you can get in most supermarkets)
Tomatoes . . . medium-sized and heirloom, preferably. Brandywines are delicious here . . . 2 or 3 depending on size

Oil-cured olives—lots of these
½ jar of capers, drained (about 3 or 4 ounces, I
  imagine)
Good blue cheese
Good thick balsamic

Tear your lovely peasant-style crusty baguette into rough cubes and coat with a little olive oil, then rub with garlic cloves and salt and pepper.

Put bread cubes on an oil-coated cookie sheet and bake for about half an hour at 350°F.

Toss your greens, arugula and mixed, and those black oily olives, and the drained capers (you might want a whole jar), and some interesting cow's-milk blue. We have a dairy here with one called Bailey Blue that would be just perfect. It is soft and creamy but not so wet that you can't crumble it.

Add your croutons (those hunks of baguette you have been baking) and tomatoes, then drizzle with that good thick balsamic you have been saving, and your summer supper on the porch is ready to eat. If you are married to a someone or you are someone who wants a little grilled meat on a balmy summer night . . . grill a tenderloin with a hard sear and plenty of salt and lots of fresh pepper to about medium . . . pink and hot in the middle . . . and slice it thinly over the salad. If you add beef you may want to add some very thinly sliced red onions too. Just about half an onion's worth should do it.

You could substitute a Chilean sea bass for another version of goodness . . . or tuna, either one . . . cook skin-side down on the grill for 30 minutes only. Again, lots of salt and more pepper . . .

You might need to get a cheap bottle of Garnacha—I love Evodia. You may wind up necking under the stars out there but so long as you have waited until mid-June the mayflies will be gone and you will have a fine time.

Summer Watermelon Salad

Here's another cheese-laden summer salad that will let you eat cheese and not feel too guilty about it either. Not like cheese grits, which maybe I won't even include, 'cause just writing about them adds on pounds.

One small watermelon
Arugula—a big bunch of it
Oil-cured black olives, pitted, about 4 ounces
Feta cheese, about 4–6 ounces
Chopped nuts, ½ cup-ish (optional)
Good balsamic for drizzling
Sea salt
Freshly ground pepper

First you buy those watermelons you saw by the side of the road. There were only four. Probably all they had. So go back and get 'em all. This recipe will help you use them up.

Cube one small to medium melon and add a big bunch of Arugula gently torn, black oily olives, and some of that amazing creamy farm-stand goat feta (it is soft and silky sweet, with just a hint of earth and maybe spice—God, it's good), also broken up. Maybe add a few chopped pecans or walnuts.

Drizzle with a little good balsamic and some sea salt and freshly ground pepper.

Oh my. That's all. Just oh my.

Oh all right, here is the easy grits recipe. But it will not be my fault if you make these one cold December morning and need new pants in a bigger size come March.

It will not.

Easy Cheddar Grits
Save this for special occasions . . . like right before a long hibernation, maybe.

1 cup instant grits (Real southerners will tell you that instant grits are a sin. But since I am not a real southerner, I won't and you will never be the wiser.)

Pint of heavy cream (You won't need it all but you might want some in your coffee, too. Why not go all the way, while you're at this?)

Bunch of scallions
Hunk of or ⅓–½ cup cheddar cheese, grated
A little good Parmesan Reggiano for sprinkling

Make a cup of grits according to the recipe on the instant box, only don't use water. Nosiree. Stir in cream. Yep, cream. Just drizzle it in a little at a time. They will soak up the cream and need more. You can use half cream and half milk or half cream and finish with half-and-half. But what you want is thick and sinfully rich. With instant, this is the only way to achieve it.

In another pan, sauté a bunch of finely chopped scallions in butter or oil.

When the grits are almost cooked through, add the scallions and the cheddar cheese. You want an aged Vermont cheddar for this. Or you could use a Cheshire from West River Creamery in Vermont called Londonderry. It is a traditional clothbound Cheshire that will make this so good you will cry. They do a farmhouse cheddar, called Cambridge, that is also rich and tangy. I get them at the farmer's market, but I bet you can get them on the web, too.

When the grits are cooked all the way through, add salt and freshly ground pepper to taste and pour everything into a pie pan. Sprinkle the Parm on top and bake in a 350°F oven for about 30 minutes, or until golden and bubbly, whichever comes sooner.

Remove it from the oven and let it settle. In a few minutes, you will be able to slice it like pie. People will think you slaved for hours. They will praise you over and over and then they will need a little nap.

EGGS

So, my old See 'n Say taught me that chickens lay eggs. It didn't say how many. Young chickens lay eggs like crazy. At least one every other day for the first two years or so. Sometimes every day. Some breeds lay more than others. The chicken books are woefully cautious about predicting this, since many people who get chickens apparently want to sell the eggs, so they need big producers. For a family, I suspect any gaggle of hens will give you more than you need. We have eleven hens and one rooster just at the moment. So we have gobs of eggs. Egg dishes have become house specialties.

Crepes

They use a lot of eggs. And they have the side benefit of feeding many hungry teenagers and being delicious.

8 eggs
4½ cups milk
4 cups flour
1 pinch salt
½ pound butter
¾ cup sugar

Lightly mix all ingredients and pour into a hot pan that has been greased with a little butter. This makes about 16 crepes in an average omelet or crepe pan.

Fill with Nutella for happy kids, and then roll them up and dust them with powdered sugar.

Adults and discerning kids will like crepes with lemon squeezed all over them while they are cooking (both sides), and then again on the plate. Roll them and dust with powdered sugar. Serve with slices of lemon.

Sometimes in summer, when we have the most eggs, I make savory crepes with ham, Gruyère, and tarragon. Use your imagination . . .

Lovely Fluffy Quiche

FOR THE CRUST
1¼ cups flour
A pinch of salt
½ cup cold sweet butter, cut into small cubes
4 tablespoons ice water, or more as needed

FOR THE CUSTARD
3 large eggs
1½ cups cream
A pinch of salt
A bit of pepper
A grating of nutmeg
1 cup grated Gruyère

FOR THE FILLING
Asparagus, broccoli, or whatever your heart
  desires

MAKE THE CRUST: Combine flour and salt.

Cut in the butter with a pastry blender, working quickly to keep the butter cold, until it is the size of small peas. (You can also use your KitchenAid mixer for this.)

Add the ice water, a tablespoon at a time, tossing with a fork until you can gather it together in a ball. You might need more than 4 tablespoons of water, but use only just as much as you need to make the dough come together.

Flatten it into a disk, wrap in wax paper, and allow to rest for an hour (or overnight) in the refrigerator.

BAKE THE CRUST: Preheat the oven to 400°F.

Roll out the dough on a floured surface and fit it into a pie pan. (You can use those tart pans with the removable bottoms but you don't have to.) Line the dough with foil and fill with dried beans for weight.

Bake for 12 to 15 minutes. It should be ready now, but if you try to remove the foil and it sticks, leave it in the oven for a couple minutes more. Then, carefully remove the weights, prick the crust gently with a fork (to avoid air bubbles), and bake for 5 minutes more, or until the crust is golden. Set it on a rack to rest for at least half an hour.

Turn the heat down to 375°F. If you're using a filling that doesn't go in the custard, like asparagus, for just one luscious example, add that to the crust now.

MAKE THE CUSTARD: Whisk the eggs, cream, and seasonings to combine, but don't froth.

Pour the mixture into the cooled tart shell. Top with grated cheese and bake for about half an hour (longer if there are other fillings), until the top is golden and puffy. It should quiver gently, barely set.

Serve immediately, before the glorious puff of the custard gives a little sigh and begins to collapse.

Yankee Deviled Eggs

Real southerners (who abound in my friend circle, for some reason) don't use sugar, and call my eggs Yankee with some real derision. But then, they eat every single one so I don't worry much about what they say.

And I am leaving out the boiling, peeling, slicing bits, as I know you know all of that already.

1 dozen old eggs . . . at least a week old (Fresh
  eggs don't peel worth a darn.)
4 scallions, finely chopped
1 tablespoon sugar
2 teaspoons-ish mayonnaise
1 teaspoon mustard
Salt and freshly ground pepper

Thoroughly mix egg yolks, scallions, sugar,
mayo, mustard, and salt and pepper.
  Refill eggs and watch the crowd gobble 'em up.
  (Add a little crisped pancetta for fancy bacon
and eggs.)

Ellen's Best Prosciutto Brioche
(very eggy dough)

*I always double this. They are good for a
crowd and they taste good hot out of the oven.
They are just as good cold for days after
making. This looks and tastes like it is much
harder to make than it actually is.*

Makes about four dozen rolls.

PASTRY
3½ cups flour
½ cup sugar
2 packages (¼ ounce each) active dry yeast
1 teaspoon grated lemon peel
½ teaspoon salt

⅔ cup butter
½ cup milk
5 eggs

FILLING
Mascarpone
Fennel seeds
1 pound of good prosciutto, diced into small
   pieces
Finely grated Gruyère

In a large mixing bowl, combine 1½ cups of the flour, sugar, yeast, lemon peel, and salt.

In a saucepan or microwave, melt butter in milk no more than 120–130°F. (So don't do this on high in the microwave or it will get too hot and separate.) Add to dry ingredients and beat until moistened.

Add eggs and beat, then add 1 cup of the flour and beat until smooth. Stir in the remaining flour but do not knead. Spoon dough into a greased bowl and cover. Let rise in a warm place for about an hour.

This will make a yellow gooey mess. Yes, it is supposed to look like this.

Gently punch dough down, cover, and refrigerate overnight. If you need this today, just put it in the freezer uncovered for an hour (or, if you are really late, for just as long as you can) and then make a few (a dozen, or however many your cookie sheet can comfortably accommodate) from the harder dough on top—putting the rest back in the freezer while that batch bakes.

Punch dough down and turn onto a lightly floured surface, unless you are using the freezer method—cut some from the dough and set the rest aside. If you are using the freezer method, just take your pieces from the hardest part of the top. Divide the dough into 16 equally sized small balls, maybe a teaspoon, and place on a parchment-lined cookie sheet that has been covered in fennel seeds.

Using your fingers, press a good-sized dab of mascarpone into the dough. Sprinkle your dough top with the Gruyère cheese. Then add 5 or 6 pieces of diced prosciutto all over the top of the cheese.

Next, gently pull a little of the stretchy dough from one side of the roll to the other. You can do this in a couple of places. It will look messy. Don't worry; it will bake beautifully. You just want a little of the stretchy dough from one side touching the stretchy dough on the other.

Sprinkle grated Gruyère all over the top. If it looks messy and there is some Gruyère on the sides and on the parchment paper, you will get those baked cheesy pieces hanging off the edges of your pastry. Don't worry. Everybody loves these.

Bake at 375°F for a few minutes, until golden brown.

TAKE HOME SUPPERS

There were so many of these . . . Whatever we wanted to eat became a Peltier's Take Home Supper, since we could save time by cooking our suppers at the store.

Benjamin was going to Green Mountain College, just half an hour away, and his friends would come by for these lots of nights. So we were always cooking for a crowd, even if they weren't always exactly customers.

Plus, we might have been headed for trouble, but we were also going to get fat! We had to get something out of it.

Here are a few favorites. Yes, despite what I said, and will say, a few people bought these all the time. And the tourists. The tourists loved them. Just because we were lousy shopkeepers didn't mean we couldn't cook.

We can definitely cook. And eat. Both of those.

HQCS Crab Cakes

So, John was sick of making these, but they really are delicious and eventually we got back to making them for ourselves. You should, too. They are really great in the summer with a skewer of grilled watermelon and pineapple on the side and a pile of fresh sliced salted heirloom tomatoes.

They are also tasty with a little bit of strawberry salsa (see chapter 4, note 1) on top.

2 tablespoons unsalted butter
2 tablespoons olive oil
¾ cup small-diced red onion (1 small onion)
1½ cups small-diced celery (4 stalks)
½ cup small-diced red bell pepper (1 small pepper)
½ cup small-diced yellow bell pepper (1 small pepper)
¼ cup minced fresh tarragon
1 tablespoon capers, drained
¼ teaspoon Tabasco sauce
½ teaspoon Worcestershire sauce
1½ teaspoons Old Bay seasoning
½ teaspoon kosher salt
½ teaspoon freshly ground black pepper

½ pound lump crabmeat, drained and picked to remove shells
½ cup plain dry bread crumbs
½ cup good mayonnaise
2 teaspoons Dijon mustard
2 extra-large eggs, lightly beaten

FOR FRYING
4 tablespoons unsalted butter
¼ cup olive oil

Place butter, olive oil, onion, celery, red and yellow bell peppers, tarragon, capers, Tabasco sauce, Worcestershire sauce, Old Bay seasoning, salt, and pepper in a large sauté pan over medium-low heat and cook until the vegetables are soft, approximately 15 to 20 minutes. Cool to room temperature.

In a large bowl, break the crabmeat into small pieces and toss with the bread crumbs, mayonnaise, mustard, and eggs.

Add the cooked mixture and mix well.

Cover and chill in refrigerator for 30 minutes.

Shape into bite-sized crab cakes.

Heat the butter and olive oil for frying over medium heat in a large sauté pan. Add the crab cakes and fry for 4 to 5 minutes on each side, until browned. Drain on paper towels; keep crab cakes warm in a 250°F oven and serve hot.

Pulled Pork Sandwiches

This one has a few steps, but it is well worth the effort. And none of it is particularly hard. This is not for when you are in a hurry.

1 12-pound boneless pork shoulder
12 soft buns

FOR THE DRY RUB
6 tablespoons paprika
4 tablespoons granulated sugar
4 tablespoons brown sugar
1 tablespoon onion powder
2 tablespoons dark cocoa powder
Kosher salt and rough ground pepper

FOR THE BARBECUE SAUCE
2 cups ketchup
1 cup water
¼ cup packed brown sugar
¼ cup sugar
1½ teaspoons fresh ground pepper
1½ teaspoons onion powder
1½ teaspoons dry mustard
2–4 tablespoons lemon juice
2 tablespoons Worcestershire sauce
½ cup good balsamic vinegar
2 tablespoons light corn syrup

RUB THE PORK: Combine dry-rub ingredients in bowl, setting aside 2 tablespoons. Apply remaining mix to pork and rub.

Cover pork with plastic wrap and refrigerate for a couple of hours or overnight if you have time.

COOK THE PORK: Place the pork fat-side down on a rack in the smoker or on the grill. Cover and cook, at 275°F, turning every hour or so, until a thermometer inserted into the center registers 165°F, about 6 hours.

MAKE THE SAUCE: Meanwhile, mix together the sauce ingredients and the reserved dry rub over high heat. Bring to a boil, stirring, then reduce the heat to low, and simmer uncovered, stirring occasionally, at least 2 hours. Let cool, then reheat on the grill when ready to use.

PULL . . . (SHRED) THE PORK: Transfer the pork to a rimmed baking sheet (you'll want to catch all the flavorful juices) and let stand until cool enough to handle. Shred into bite-size pieces, pile on a platter, and pour any juices from the baking sheet on top.

MAKE THE SANDWICHES: Mound the pork on bun bottoms, paint with a little BBQ sauce, top with slaw if you like, and cover with the bun tops. Best sandwich ever!

Strawberry Soup

This is a great dessert, very elegant in small, squat crystal bowls or glasses, and it is a fabulous brunch or lunch soup.

It has amazingly deep flavors for something that you just mix and chill. This will make you happy for the rest of your life. I promise.

4 cups strawberries, cleaned
½ cup sugar
¼ cup white wine
1½ cups heavy cream . . . (worry about calories some other day)
3 cups apple juice
Juice of 1 lemon
½ cup honey
1½ cups buttermilk

Put the berries in a food processor and give a rough chop. Add all else. Chill in giant bowl in fridge for at least two hours till a little fizzy.

Braised Short Ribs

Serve with a good Beaujolais cru for a soft, warm feeling of contentment that will get you through winter down to about minus-ten degrees. After that, nothing much helps.

3 pounds boneless beef short ribs
A little bit of good olive oil
1 cup beef stock
⅓ cup good balsamic vinegar
½ cup dark cocoa
¼ cup honey
2 or 3 garlic cloves, minced
Few cayenne pepper flakes
Lots of tarragon
1 cup (ish) red wine

Mix all ingredients, except meat, and simmer. Sear the ribs in the olive oil on very high heat for a deep brown color and then put into simmering pot. Bring to a boil, then reduce heat and simmer till tender . . . couple of hours, usually.

Serve on top of cheddar grits for a deeply rich and satisfying winter meal.

Moroccan Shepherd's Pie

This is just really simple and good. Every kid everywhere will eat this and ask for it again and again. Grownups like it, too.

1 whole chicken (Cheat with a market rotisserie chicken and you can be done in a flash.)
2 onions
⅓ cup honey
⅓ cup dark cocoa powder
½ cup chicken stock
¼ cup fresh tarragon
Good sea salt
Freshly ground black pepper . . .
Garlic powder . . .
Onion powder . . .
Cinnamon . . . (a little of each . . . maybe a half teaspoon, but mostly just to taste)
A little nutmeg . . . maybe a teaspoon
2 tablespoons good thick balsamic
1 cup hearty red wine
Parmesan cheese, grated

Boil the chicken and shred the meat. Set aside.
Sauté onions in your favorite oil until light and translucent. Add remaining ingredients, except for the cheese. Bring to a boil and add the shredded chicken.
Cover with mashed potatoes (Yukon gold

make the best mashed . . . and use real butter, would you? The trick to perfect mashed potatoes every time is to melt the butter in the milk before adding to the potatoes). Cover with a little shredded Parm and bake for about 45 minutes at 350°F.

Homemade Pizza

Because it is so much better, and simple besides. (I tripled this for the seven pizzas we produced the other night.)

2 cups flour
⅔ cup warm water
½ teaspoon salt
2 teaspoons yeast

Yeast proof . . . mix with a little of the warm water and a teaspoon of sugar and let rise atop stove. If you turn your oven on you can speed this up a little. Takes 15–30 minutes.

Mix all ingredients and knead for 7–10 minutes. Let rise until doubled, approximately 2 hours.

SPECIAL TOPPINGS: Mascarpone, layer of fig comfit or heavy fig jam, layer of prosciutto . . . sprinkle fresh black pepper, Parmesan Reggiano, and serve. People will beg you for this recipe. Or try mascarpone, a little garlic powder, and peas. This one is amazing. Really. I swear. Try it.

Also, fresh tomatoes, basil, and fresh mozzarella atop regular pizza sauce is really good.

For the regular pizza sauce I add approximately two teaspoons sugar and 1½ tablespoons of cinnamon per jar if using store bought . . . maybe a little garlic too.

Prebake dough in a 500°F oven for about 5 minutes. Buy a pizza stone if you can, which makes it cook more evenly. Sprinkle your stone with cornmeal for easy removal of crusts. Repeat after every two or three pizzas.

When using regular tomato sauce, place it mainly in the middle.

It will spread during baking.

Bake for about 3–5 minutes at 500°F until bubbly.

The Vermonter

We made these outside the store during our annual autumn festival. When it was sunny and orange, we had musicians, caramel apples, and horse-drawn carriage rides and sold bunches of them. When it rained and practically nobody came, we assuaged our misery by eating lots of them ourselves.

Either way, they are delicious.

Grilled panini with thick-cut ham, whatever apples you picked that week, and good, really sharp local Vermont cheddar.

Soak the apples in a little maple syrup for two hours in the fridge. Layer it all—cheddar, ham, apples, ham, cheddar—on good rye, and grill.

CHRISTMAS SEASON SNACKS

I believe in the goodness of sugar and butter, especially at Christmas. The gooeyer the better. Here are a few of the foods we have around every December. There are so many special foods we enjoy that time of year; these are just some of the standard snacks. If I don't make them at the same general time they're expected every year, I get a revolt.

Food is sort of the bass note of the songs around here. The melody changes some, but the bass is always there keeping the beat.

Chocolate Peanut Butter Balls

I make these over and over every year in December. You simply have to have them for Christmas Adventure weekend. Eli and all his friends always want these every day after school just before the holiday break. And I love to accommodate them. We have to have a pile of them when we wrap presents, and every year at our big winter party, if folks don't see them they will ask. Plus, of course they have to be on the table on the actual day, and there had better be plenty for the next week too. One year, during the worst of the

HQCS, I gained nine pounds in December alone. I credit these delicious little menaces.

They are not complicated. But they do take time. Worth it, though, since the people you make them for will worship you.

A pound of peanut butter (I prefer all creamy. Some people use half crunchy, half creamy.)

½ cup butter

2½ cups powdered sugar

3 cups Rice Krispies (These must be fresh. And I think they're essential. They add a bit of depth.)

1 package chocolate chips, semisweet

¼ bar of paraffin wax (You can use just a bit of Crisco if you don't have—or prefer not to use—paraffin. If you're gifting these, paraffin is kind of essential. If not, you can really leave it out and be okay. It won't be as pretty, but you don't have eyeballs in your stomach! If you use only ¼ bar you will not taste it and they will look lovely.)

Mix together the peanut butter, butter, powdered sugar, and Rice Krispies. Stir, stir, stir. Form into small balls. Smaller than PingPong balls. Maybe about bouncy-ball size. Put them in the freezer.

While the inside is becoming a hard little middle of love, get out your double boiler, choco chips, and paraffin wax. (No double broiler? No problem. Fill a big pan with water and set a smaller pan on top. Voila! You have a double broiler.) Melt the chocolate and paraffin together. Without the paraffin wax, the candy won't get quite as hard and therefore will become somewhat of a messy disaster when you eat them. Which is no big deal if you are just eating the batch yourself.

Take out the frozen balls and use a wooden skewer to dip the peanut butter goodness into the chocolate deliciousness. You may want to keep about half of them in the freezer—otherwise they get a bit soft and the dipping becomes more like dropping them into the pot and picking them out with a spoon. (Not that I've ever done that.)

After you've dunked each ball, let it sit on wax paper for a while and harden. You can speed this up by putting them in the fridge. You'll probably eat a few while they wait and that is okay. You are just testing them for the fam.

John's Grandmother's Roszke Cookies

I married him for her bread, and then I got cookies, too. John had these every Christmas and Easter throughout his childhood. I asked Grandma to teach me when I married him so he could have them the rest of his life, too. Now they are also a Christmas memory for all of our kids and our friends. Grandma

Rimarchik's sweet Slovak brand of love lives on in her recipes. That is not a bad legacy, come to think of it.

FOR THE DOUGH
6 egg yolks
½ pound butter (Not margarine. Margarine wasn't invented when this recipe was and ruins it.)
2 tablespoons lard (Crisco works)
6 tablespoons powdered sugar
4 cups flour
½ pint sour cream
1 teaspoon salt
2½ teaspoons dry yeast

FOR THE FILLING
2 pounds finely chopped pecans
2 egg whites, beaten
Sugar and cinnamon to taste

Cream eggs and shortening. Add sugar, gradually add flour, add sour cream. Melt yeast in ¼ cup warm milk—add to mixture. Work dough (add flour if tacky). Refrigerate overnight.

Take out in morning and let sit for half hour. Work it. Cut in 8 or 9 pieces. Work them. Roll into balls. Let rise half hour and roll and cut into squares. Spread filling over square and then roll like crescents. Let rise half hour after filled. Bake for 20–25 minutes at 350°F. Roll in powdered sugar and cinnamon when cool.

Cheese Ball

This is practically right out of The Brady Bunch. *It is such a bad-looking thing and it is absolutely compelling. Guests sneer a little and pretty soon they taste it and then they can't stop. If you are over forty, this will make you very happy. If you are younger than that, rent some DVDs of '70s TV sitcoms like* Love, American Style *and* The Partridge Family *to get yourself in the mood.*

8 ounces cream cheese
8 ounces sharp cheddar
1 jar of Spanish olives, finely chopped
Some celery seed
Some garlic powder
A little celery salt
Several splashes of Worcestershire
Pecans, finely minced

Mix all and roll into a ball before rolling in the minced pecans.

Chill for about four hours before serving with basic Ritz crackers for authentic 1970s party food.

Lobster Mac 'n Cheese

I make these ahead in little ramekins and freeze them. Throughout the holidays, anytime someone drops in I can thaw them in the microwave and bake and it seems like I am a kitchen genius. These are also great for the day after.

8 ounces elbow macaroni
16 ounces cream or whole milk
8 ounces shredded sharp white cheddar
6 ounces fresh Parmesan cheese, grated
4 ounces mascarpone
4 ounces Gruyère cheese
1 pound cooked lobster meat, shredded (You can order lobster tails from your fish market in prepackaged bags. You may need to shred it more thoroughly.)
½ cup breadcrumbs, chopped
2 garlic cloves, minced
2 big shallots, minced
1 tablespoon olive oil
Salt and pepper to taste

Bring salted water to a boil and add macaroni. Cook 8 to 10 minutes (do not overcook). In a double boiler, combine the cheddar cheese, 4 ounces of the Parmesan cheese, the mascarpone, and Gruyère cheeses and heat until well blended.

I gradually add the cream or milk along the way so that it is really smooth. Mix with the pasta.

Pour into ramekins and sprinkle the bread-crumbs on top with the leftover Parm.

Bake at 350°F till bubbly.

Karen's Stromboli

Great for the day before, when everyone is wrapping presents, or the day after, when nobody wants to cook or sit at a table but everybody wants to nosh. This recipe makes enough for one stromboli; make extra and freeze.

FOR THE DOUGH
2 cups bread flour
1 teaspoon instant or rapid-rise yeast
¾ teaspoon salt
2 tablespoons olive oil (plus extra for the bowl)
1 cup warm water

FOR THE FILLING
1 pound thinly sliced spicy capicola
½ pound sliced provolone
(You can really use anything, as long as it is not wet. The original recipe calls for jarred roasted red peppers—dried and chopped—but if using spicy capicola, it is enough spice. If using ham or

a salami, you can add spice by sprinkling with dried red pepper flakes.)

PREPARE THE DOUGH: Pulse the flour, yeast, and salt in a food processor with a dough blade. With the food processor running, pour in the oil, then the water, and process until a rough ball forms (about 30 seconds).

Let the dough rest for 2 minutes, then process for another 30 seconds.

Turn out into a lightly floured work surface and knead by hand to form a smooth ball (about 5 minutes), adding flour as needed to keep the dough from sticking.

Transfer to a lightly oiled bowl, cover with plastic wrap, and let rise until doubled (about an hour).

Deflate the dough with your fist and turn it out onto an unfloured work surface; reshape into a ball.

Spray plastic wrap with spray oil and wrap and let rest for 15 minutes before rolling and filling.

ASSEMBLE: On a lightly floured work surface, roll the dough into a rectangle about ¼ inch thick.

Place a layer of meat, a layer of cheese, and another layer of meat on the dough, leaving a 1-inch border. Brush the edges with water, roll into a cylinder, pressing the edges to seal.

You can wrap in plastic wrap and refrigerate (for 24 hours) or freeze at this point.

BAKE: Place on a cookie sheet lined with parchment paper, seam-side down. If frozen, thaw before baking.

Brush with egg.

Spray or drizzle aluminum foil with oil and lay loosely over top of the stromboli. Bake at 350°F for 25 minutes, remove tinfoil and bake another 20 minutes until golden.

COMFORT FOOD

Loaded Mashed Potatoes
What to eat when the lady drives off with your gas pump and you're going broke . . .

2 heads garlic
6 pounds Idaho potatoes, peeled and quartered
Salt
2 teaspoons freshly ground black pepper
½ cup butter
1 (12 ounce) carton sour cream
1 (8 ounce) block aged sharp white Vermont cheddar, grated
1½ pounds cooked pancetta, julienned

Preheat oven to 350°F.

Cut tops off garlic heads. Wrap in foil and roast for 30 minutes. When cool enough to handle, remove flesh from garlic heads and set aside.

In a large stockpot, cook potatoes in enough salted water to cover for 10 to 15 minutes or until tender. Drain and return to stockpot. Beat with an electric mixer until smooth, adding salt to taste, pepper, butter, the roasted garlic, and sour cream. With a spatula, stir in cheese and pancetta. Add more salt and pepper, if necessary. Serve immediately.

Going broke is fattening.

This next little recipe is the kind of food you eat the day the "workout" guy from the bank shows up. You eat this the first time, and then every time you have to call him to ask him to raise the credit limit on your checking account.

My friend Karen brought these over when Benjamin had ankle surgery. She brought them again one day when I was crying about the store. She brought them when we finally decided to sell the store and couldn't find a buyer, too. Finally she just sent me the recipe.

Karen's Satisfying Comforting Potatoes

The recipe calls for 10 potatoes—I use about 6 huge ones. I also use 4½ cups aged white sharp Vermont cheddar in the potatoes and 2 cups slightly milder cheddar on top, mixed with a little good Parmesan Reggiano.

10 Russet or other good baking potatoes
1 stick butter
1 cup sour cream
½ cup heavy cream
¾ pound cooked bacon, chopped
½ pound sharp Vermont cheddar, grated
½ cup green onions, sliced
3 eggs
¾ pound mild cheddar

Bake the potatoes at 350°F for an hour, or until fork-tender.

Cool, and remove skins; cut up.

Mix all the ingredients except the mild cheddar in a bowl and blend. Put in a casserole dish.

Top with the mild cheddar. Bake at 350°F for 30–35 minutes.

ROMANTIC COMFORT FOOD
(for when you need a little of both)

Sage Tagliatelle

First light a whole bunch of candles out on the porch . . .

1 pound pancetta
3 or 4 fat bunches of sage
About 1 pound tagliatelle
Mascarpone
Good Parmesan Reggiano, grated
Fresh eggs

Crisp the pancetta. Add the sage in the last couple of minutes and sauté lightly.

Cook the pasta al dente in well-salted water and toss lightly with mascarpone and the pancetta and sage.

Fry egg fast and place on top of each serving to sauce, with a little pepper and a scattering of the Parm.

Sit outside and remember you chose all of this and, luckily, you are still glad you did.

❧ In Memoriam ❧

Eloise

Eloise had a sweet, peaceful death, with all five of us holding her and telling her how much we loved her. We sat out on the porch, and the vet sat with us for a little while. Everyone cried and petted and hugged her one last time.

The decision seems clearer, in retrospect. Bone cancer had reduced her life to a couple of trips outside that took forever to accomplish, and the occasional room change during the day. She was ready to go even if we weren't ready to let her go. The increasing dosages of pain meds had stopped working.

She elegantly gave the vet her paw for the shot, and I held her in my arms as she died. Our vet had brought an assistant, and the two of them wrapped her in a lovely old quilt. We kissed her one more time, and they carried her solemnly like the best, most gentle pallbearers to the back seat of their car. Her ashes were bound for the flower garden.

Eloise was a big part of this family. She was calm and steady. If one of the kids yelled or wrestled too hard with another, she would correct them with one bark and a gentle restraining

Berner bump. She insisted on good manners. Her quiet elegance was a model for this loud, rambunctious, unruly group of ours. She was like having a sweet maiden auntie from another era around to remind us all to behave.

She had the biggest vocabulary of any dog I have ever known. She was brainy and beautiful, and everyone who met her was smitten. She exuded a soulful, gentle love that calmed and gentled colicky babies and grumpy adults alike.

We loved her deeply and will miss her enormously, but we are ever grateful to have had the time.

Eloise Rushing Stimson
December 10, 1998–
May 12, 2009

Stuart

Hannah and I saw him in a mall pet store while we waited to pick up her eyeglasses. I would never buy a puppy from a pet store, and by doing so encourage the puppy mills that flourished in the Midwest.

Nosiree, not me.

But little kids love to look in pet stores, and Hannah was no exception. We spent an hour looking at this little red-brindle Cairn Terrier curled up in his food dish. I could barely tear her away. He was adorable. But we didn't really need another dog. We had a new baby, which was plenty.

For the next two weeks, I couldn't stop thinking about him. I'd never wanted a terrier, and besides, we'd just had Eli. How could I even be thinking about a puppy?

Only, then I had the dream. In this dream, our house was on fire, and that little terrier was barking, sounding the alarm. He woke us up just in time to get the kids out of the house. I told John, when I woke up, that I had to go and buy that puppy.

He said, "Hon, it's been over two weeks. He is probably long gone by now."

I called the store that day and, of course, since

it was meant to be, he was still there. He barked incessantly when we played with him in the puppy room. He writhed when we tried to cuddle him and jumped right out of our arms. He was squirmy and loud. John deadpanned that maybe it wasn't a love match.

But there had been that dream. I was undeterred.

We bought a book about Cairns, and drove off with the loud bundle. John offered that maybe he just needed a proper Scottish name. So we called him Stuart, and he became ours.

The loud little rat did eventually settle down, and when he did, he became the heart of our family. He and Eli were like littermates. They slept together curled in one sweet ball for about the next seven years. Eli told anyone who asked from ages two till about six that he had two brothers and a sister. Stuart was his other brother. We buried bones under our deck in St. Louis, where he would dig happily for hours in the cool dirt.

He was always our protector. I would kiss him goodbye when I left town for business, and tell him to keep an eye on things. I would swear to God, he saluted.

"Sargent Stu on duty. Don't worry, Mom, I've got the ball."

The sadness and worry of the tougher days did not escape him, so John became his job just like

Eli had been when he was little. He followed John everywhere.

Somehow he even figured out where John went at five every morning. Many mornings, when I got up and let him out, he would wander down to the store and wait for someone to let him inside, where he would have a bone and help greet the customers.

How did he know? It was his job.

Fifteen years is a long time for a dog. His eyes grew cataracts and his diet changed to scrambled eggs and chicken and rice. He took on the smell of an old man no matter how many times we bathed him in coconut soap. It got hard for him to stay on the path that last year, but he never tired of walking the perimeter of our land. It just took him longer. John dug long paths in the snow for him that last winter, and he would sort of waddle around sniffing, making sure everything was all right. He got to meet Oscar, and then he turned the reins over to Corporal Pippi, who has guarded us since.

We miss him still. And I will always be grateful. Thanks, Stu.

Stuart Rushing Stimson
September 1, 1995–
September 17, 2010

Sophie

Sophie, our sweet tabby, was here for all of it. We stole her at a picnic in St. Louis when Benjamin was just a toddler. We were at John's mom's for Memorial Day. Sophie "belonged" to the neighbors. I put that heavily in quotes, because here was this little tiny wild kitten, about eight weeks old, left outside and alone, while her family spent the holiday at Six Flags.

I ask you. For all I knew their kids were locked in the garage.

Sophie came over to our picnic, where a bit of washed-off pork steak thrilled her. She ate like she was starving. And, you know how cats never drink much? She lapped up an entire saucer of water. That sealed it as far as Benjamin was concerned. Me, too, of course. There was never really any choice.

We stole her.

So Sophie, quickly adopted and named by our three-year-old Benjamin, lived with us in our hip St. Louis Lafayette Square walk-up. She watched over a sleeping infant Hannah in our first sweet little house, in Edwardsville, Illinois. And she cheerfully came along to our next St. Louis life. She followed us less cheerfully, it must be said, on the plane bound for Vermont. (It was the crowded TSA hassle that made her grumpy.)

She had seen it all. And even in her eighteenth year, she meowed hello at each and every one of us each and every morning.

She died as she came to us, surrounded by Benjamin, John, and me. We held her and loved her and told the happy stories of her life.

We are all better because Sophie loved us.

Sophie Rushing Stimson
April 1, 1988–
February 17, 2006

※ Acknowledgments ※

Big thanks and loud, messy love to my John, Benjamin, Hannah, and Eli—who are all probably long accustomed to being fodder for my stories, but maybe not quite like this.

Also I thank Todd Porter at Porter Collected Works. He was a patient and funny editor and, even better, a good friend.

And thanks to Rosalie Siegel, my opinionated, smart, fabulous agent. She claims she is retiring but just let me see her try.

And to all my friends at Norton and Countryman, who just kept saying yes.

☞ About the Author ☜

Ellen Stimson lives in a beautiful old farmhouse nestled in a high valley in the mountains of Vermont with her wild pack of children, not-so-wild husband, and completely civilized group of chickens, sheep, dogs, and cats. She has a not-at-all-fashionable collection of muck boots. This is her first book.

Center Point Large Print
600 Brooks Road / PO Box 1
Thorndike ME 04986-0001 USA

(207) 568-3717

US & Canada:
1 800 929-9108
www.centerpointlargeprint.com